THE IDEA OF PHENOMENOLOGY

EDMUND HUSSERL

THE IDEA OF
PHENOMENOLOGY

Translated by

WILLIAM P. ALSTON

AND

GEORGE NAKHNIKIAN

Introduction by

GEORGE NAKHNIKIAN

THE HAGUE

MARTINUS NIJHOFF

1964

PREFACE

This translation is concluded in our *Readings in Twentieth-Century Philosophy*, (N.Y., The Free Press of Glencoe, Inc., 1963). We owe thanks to Professors W. D. Falk and William Hughes for helping us with the translation. We also owe thanks to Professor Herbert Spiegelberg, Dr. Walter Biemel and the Husserl Archives at Louvain for checking it and we are especially indebted to Professor Dorion Cairns, many of whose suggestions we incorporated in the final draft.

WILLIAM P. ALSTON
GEORGE NAKHNIKIAN

January 1964

CONTENTS

INTRODUCTION

From April 26 to May 2, 1907, Husserl delivered five lectures in Göttingen. They introduce the main ideas of his later phenomenology, the one that goes beyond the phenomenology of the *Logische Untersuchungen*. These lectures and Husserl's summary of them entitled "The Train of Thoughts in the Lectures" were edited by Dr. Walter Biemel and first published in 1950 under the title *Die Idee der Phänomenologie*.[1] Husserl wrote the summary on the night of the last lecture, not for formal delivery but for his own use. This accounts for the fact that the summary contains incomplete sentences. There are some discrepancies between Lecture V and the corresponding passages in the summary. We may suppose that the passages in the summary are a closer approximation to what Husserl wanted to say.

This introduction is an attempt to explain the significance of these Göttingen lectures in Husserl's philosophical development.

To the student reared in the English-speaking tradition in philosophy, Husserl's phenomenology may seem bizarre. But the same student will have no trouble seeing that Husserl is squarely in the mainstream of recent philosophy in one important respect. A dominant and recurring motif in recent philosophical thought is the conviction that philosophy is not a factual science, it cannot ground itself in the findings of the factual sciences, and it cannot use the methods of investigation characteristic of the factual sciences. This much binds together thinkers as different from one another in other respects as the logical positivists and

[1] *Husserliana* – Edmund Husserl, *Gesammelte Werke. Auf Grund des Nachlasses veröffentlicht mit dem Husserl-Archiv an der Universität Köln vom Husserl-Archiv (Louvain) unter Leitung von* H. L. Van Breda, Band II: *Die Idee der Phänomenologie. Fünf Vorlesungen, herausgegeben von* Walter Biemel, Haag, Martinus Nijhoff, 1950, 2. *Auflage* 1958.

Moore, Russell and Sartre, Wittgenstein and Heidegger, Bergson and Husserl. In Husserl's case, this motif finds expression in his attack on psychologism and in his conception of philosophy as phenomenology.

Husserl's phenomenology is an outgrowth of his attack on psychologism. Psychologism is a species of the view that philosophy is reducible to a factual science, in this case to psychology. Husserl is just as strongly against "biologism" and "anthropologism" as he is against psychologism. His critique of psychologism first appeared in 1900, in the prolegomena to the six essays in the *Logische Untersuchungen*. Prior to this, in 1891, in *The Philosophy of Arithmetic* Husserl himself had endorsed psychologism. So that in 1900, Husserl is also criticizing himself as he had been in 1891, much as Wittgenstein in the *Investigations* criticizes the earlier ideas of the *Tractatus*.

To put it more exactly, psychologism is the attempt to reduce the fundamental laws or rules of logic and mathematics to psychological generalizations about the ways in which people actually think. Take the statement:

(1) If all men are mortal and Socrates is a man, then Socrates is mortal.

A psychologistic rendering of (1) is:

(2) As a matter of fact, anyone who believes that all men are mortal and that Socrates is a man will inevitably believe that Socrates is mortal.

This is likening (1) to a scientific generalization such as one of the laws of motion. The trouble with this interpretation is that it simply does not account for the difference in the sort of certainty between (1) and (2). No one can be sure that (2) is true, unless he has made many observations, and even at that he will have only a certain degree of probability, a practical certainty, but not the absolute certainty that (1) seems to inspire. Of course, if the only difference was this difference in "feel," we could not prove anything either way. But there are explanations of why (1) inspires the certainty that it does. Husserl's explanation, one which few philosophers in the English-speaking tradition would accept as either complete or illuminating, is that *pure rational intuition* reveals that the complex *all men being mortal and Socrates being a man* comprehends the fact that Socrates is mortal. To get at this logical "fact," says Husserl, we need no empirical observation such as we need if we are ever to know whether (2) is true. Suppose we did find a man who said that he believed the complex but not what the complex is said to comprehend. Husserl would say of such a man that he was simply unreasonable. Husserl would not allow that the possibility of finding such a man would in any way refute (1). A psychologistic philosopher might next try to interpret (1) as:

(3) Anyone who believes that all men are mortal and Socrates is a man will inevitably believe that Socrates is mortal, provided that he reasons in accordance with the laws of thought.

Against this Husserl says that the notion of laws of thought is ambiguous. It can mean the matter-of-fact regularities exhibited by human thinking or it can mean the standards that determine whether a man is thinking as he ought to think. In the former sense of "laws of thought," (3) is an empirical (psychological) generalization, and it is not equivalent to (1) for the same reasons that (2) is not equivalent to (1). In the latter sense of "laws of thought," (3) is not equivalent to (2), but then (3) is not a psychological statement either.

Husserl also has arguments which, he thinks, will dispose of psychologism wholesale. He argues that any theory that reduces logic to psychology is viciously circular. We cannot derive (deduce, infer, conclude) anything from anything unless we employ some rules of inference. In other words, we cannot reason in psychology without presupposing some rule of logic or other; in fact, we cannot reason at all, in any subject matter, unless we use the laws of logic. Or, to say the same thing in still another way, we cannot *derive* any rule of logic without assuming the rules of logic.

Husserl also criticizes psychologistic theories of evidence (see, for example, Lecture IV of *The Idea of Phenomenology*, below). Here he finds the same sorts of difficulties as occur in psychologism as such. Evidence, according to Husserl, consists neither in the degree of conviction with which we believe, nor in the strength of our feelings, nor in our inclinations to take for granted. The evident is that which discloses itself to pure intuition, and evidence consists of self-givenness.

What Husserl says about the logical relations among statements he also says about the logical relations among concepts. For instance, (4) "All cats are mammals" is an "analytic" statement. It is necessarily true, and its truth is determined by the logical relation obtaining between the concept of being a cat and the concept of being a mammal. According to Husserl, an intuitive grasp of the cat concept reveals that being a mammal is necessarily involved in being a cat. Husserl divides *a priori* judgments into those that are analytic and those that are synthetic. The judgment is *a priori* if the object of the judgment does not have to be given in a perception. In the analytic judgment what is predicated of the object is "contained" in the subject-determination, that is, the predicate does not introduce anything materially new. In the synthetic *a priori* judgment, the predicated determinations are not "contained" in those of the subject; still, they are necessarily connected with them and are known to be so connected. The interested reader may study the original [1]; for a lengthy exposition in English, see Marvin Farber's *The Foundation of Phenomenology*. [2]

Thus, both in the case of logical relations among statements and among concepts, we are dealing with "essences," "universals," "abstract" entities, these being the sorts of entities that are not identified with perceptual objects. They are given to pure intuition, provided that "intuition" is not understood in the Kantian sense. In what sense, then, are we to understand it?

The answer comes in two stages, corresponding to the two stages in the development of Husserl's phenomenology. At the earlier stage of the *Logische Untersuchungen* intuition is a direct inspection of the essence of this or that type of mental act, for example, seeing, imagining, believing. Phenomenology is at this stage "descriptive psychology," differing from empirical psychology in that the latter is concerned with causal explanation but

[1] Edmund Husserl, "Bericht über deutsche Schriften zur Logik in den Jahren 1895–99," *Archiv f. syst. Phil.*, IX (1903).

[2] Marvin Farber, *The Foundation of Phenomenology*, Cambridge, Mass., Harvard University Press, 1943, chap. VI.

not with describing the essence of types of psychological acts, whereas phenomenology is concerned with describing types of psychological acts, but not with causal explanation. There is as yet no machinery of phenomenological and transcendental reduction. In the later stage of phenomenology, heralded by *The Idea of Phenomenology*, these reductions give the concept of "intuition" a new slant. "Intuition" is still to be understood in the Cartesian sense of a direct awareness of what is given, but with important modifications in both method and application.

The Idea of Phenomenology marks the transition from Husserl's earlier phenomenology in the *Investigations* to the later more radically Husserlian phenomenology. In these lectures Husserl introduces for the first time many of the major themes of his later phenomenology. These include: phenomenological reduction (the ἐποχή, the phenomenological "bracketing out"), eidetic abstraction, the pure phenomenon, the different kinds of immanence and transcendence, and the theory about the "constitution" of objects of cognition.

According to Walter Biemel, the editor of the German edition of the five lectures, Husserl underwent a crisis in the year 1906.[1] He was then having doubts about his own philosophical importance. These doubts were compounded by his failure to be appointed full professor in Göttingen. Biemel intimates that these five lectures were the beginning of a new phase, the characteristically Husserlian phenomenology, a phase initiated by Husserl's determination to take stock of himself as a philosopher. The task he set himself was no less than the critique of theoretical and practical reason. The Kantian statement of the problem suggests that Husserl was preoccupied by the same sorts of problems that plagued Kant. Husserl, however, found more inspiration in Descartes and Brentano than he did in Kant.

From Brentano, his teacher, Husserl had absorbed the intentional theory of mind.[2] According to it, intentionality characterizes mental acts such as judgments, beliefs, meanings, valu-

---

[1] See editor's Introduction to *Die Idee der Phänomenologie* (Husserliana II), The Hague, Nijhoff, 1958, 2nd ed.

[2] For comparison in the details of Brentano's, Husserl's, and the scholastic theory of intentionality, see Herbert Spiegelberg, "Der Begriff der Intentionalität in der Scholastic, bei Brentano und bei Husserl," *Philosophische Hefte*, Prag-Dejvice, vol. V, pp. 75–95. Also, Marvin Farber (see note 2, p. XII).

ations, desires, loves, hatreds, and so on. An intentional act, said Brentano, is always "about" or "of." I think of or about. I desire this or that. And the peculiarity of intentional acts is that their objects do not *have* to exist. An intentional act may have as its object an existentially mind-dependent entity, for example, the *idea* of a mermaid; or its object may be something physical; or it may be an impossible thing' such as the round square; or it may be something possible but unactualized, such as a golden mountain. Any mode of mentality (loving, desiring, believing) may have as its object an "intentionally inexistent" entity, namely, an entity that is neither physical nor existentially mind-dependent. The *idea* of a mermaid is, being an *idea*, existentially mind-dependent. But the *mermaid* which is the intention of the idea is neither a physical thing nor is it existentially mind-dependent. In contrast to this, no physical action requiring an object can be performed upon an intentionally inexistent entity. Kicking a football requires a football; but thinking of a football does not. I may think of a football that never existed. Brentano identified the mental with any intentional state, that is, with any state that *could* be directed to an intentionally inexistent entity.* Some such conception of the mental is presupposed in the *Logische Untersuchungen*.

The essences studied in the early phase of phenomenology are unreduced. In the later phenomenology these unreduced objects give way to phenomenologically and transcendentally reduced and eidetically abstracted pure phenomena present to conscious-

---

* This, however, is only one possible interpretation of Brentano's view of intentionality as presented in Chapter I of *Psychologie vom empirischen Standpunkt*.[1] It is also possible to interpret Brentano as saying that on *every* occasion of a mental act, whether there be a physical thing as referent or not, there is an intentionally inexistent entity; so that, for example, when I desire the apple in front of me, the apple is the object of my desire in one sense of "object," namely, as the thing that could satisfy my desire; but there is also another object, the intentionally inexistent apple which is the common and peculiar element in all desires of apples. My colleague, Robert Sleigh, Jr., suggested the following analogy that would be helpful to those familiar with the sense-datum theory. The sense-datum is to the intentionally inexistent object what the perceptual object, if there is one, is to the material referent, if there is one, of the intentional act. There are Brentano scholars who believe that the second interpretation is what Brentano intended. Husserl's work, at least from the *Idea of Phenomenology* on, strongly suggests that his conception of the mental is in line with the second interpretation. See also R. M. Chisholm, *Perceiving*.[2]

[1] English translation in R. M. Chisholm, *Realism and the Background of Phenomenology*, N,Y., The Free Press of Glencoe, Inc., 1960.

[2] R. M. Chisholm, *Perceiving*, Ithaca, Cornell University Press, 1957.

ness. They are essences and they are intentionally inexistent objects. Descartes's method of doubt, says Husserl, is the exactly
right *beginning* toward locating the objects of philosophical,
namely, phenomenological, inquiry. In *The Idea of Phenomenology*
Husserl avers that the problem for the critique of knowledge is
to locate the absolutely bare, presuppositionless data on which
to build the whole of knowledge; more precisely, the problem is
to intuit the essence of knowledge, and thereby to "see" how
valid cognition is an unquestionable fact. But, says Husserl,
Descartes did not use the method of doubt to the end to which it
is eminently suited, namely, to locate the pure data required by
the critique of knowledge. Even worse, Husserl implies, Descartes
misconceived the problem of knowledge. Let me try to explain
what I think Husserl has in mind.

The problem of knowledge, as Descartes posed it, simply comes
to this. How can I, the critical philosopher, justify my "natural"
beliefs about the existence and nature of all sorts of entities, from
God to the kitchen sink, entities which, by hypothesis, are not
given to me "immediately"? How can I validly move from that
which is immanent to that which is transcendent, from that
which is a content of a *cogitatio*, of a mental act, to that which lies
outside a *cogitatio*? The Cartesian method of doubt, Husserl
suggests, requires that we locate pure data, themselves independent of all presuppositions and logically adequate for the
critical reconstruction of knowledge.

According to Husserl, however, we shall fail to locate what we
need if we equate the immanent with that which is "in me" and
the transcendent with that which is "outside of me." Thus, if we
say that the content of the Cartesian *cogitatio* is a psychological
ingredient in it, a "piece of furniture" located "in me," and the
transcendent is a *different* reality existing "outside of me," then
we reduce to paradox the theory that the contents of the mind
are reliable indexes, veridical representations, of the entirely
different (because extramental) transcendencies that our empirical and *a priori* knowledge is supposed to be about. The paradox
is that, according to the theory, in order to validate knowledge
we must see that the mental content veridically represents the
extramental reality. But, as Berkeley asked, how can we ever
compare a mental content with something that, by hypothesis, is

never itself given? Descartes resorted to God to validate our "natural" beliefs. Apart from the inconclusiveness of the arguments for God's existence and the suspicion of circularity that this part of Descartes's procedure arouses, God can be used for diametrically opposed purposes: witness Berkeley. Whereas Descartes had argued that God's existence and goodness are incompatible with the nonexistence of material substance, Berkeley argued that the contrary is the case. The perceptive reader will see that according to the above, which is my interpretation of some things Husserl says about "epistemology" leading to scepticism and paradox (see *The Idea of Phenomenology*), Descartes himself would be one of the sceptical "epistemologists."

Now in the *Untersuchungen* there is no problem about justifying our "natural" belief in the independent reality of the world. The phenomenology of 1901 is not interested either in the actual existence or in the transcendently posited characteristics of things. It is interested only in their status as "phenomena" for consciousness. For example, in analyzing seeing as a mental act phenomenology (descriptive psychology) is to concern itself not with the question of the actual existence of the object seen but rather with the question of what an object would *have to be* in order to be an object for seeing. It would have to have color, hence extension, shape, size, and so on. These features would be the essence of being a visible object even if there were no actually existing colored or extended things. Later, in the post-1907 period, Husserl did worry about the problem of the independent reality of bodies and other minds, but not even then did he pose the problem in the manner that Berkeley found objectionable in Descartes.

Beginning with *The Idea of Phenomenology*, the first task of the critique of knowledge is to locate the pure data of phenomenological inquiry. To get at them, Husserl submits, we have first to notice that there are two sorts of immanences with their correlative transcendencies. On the one hand, the immanent-transcendent dichotomy covers the precritical dualism, "in me — outside of me." The crucial sense of immanence, on the other hand, is the sense in which it is intentionally inexistent essences that are immanent. They are the referents of intentional acts. Their immanence consists in their self-givenness (*Selbstgegebenheit*) to pure intuition. At the same time, they are transcendent in that their nature and reality are independent of their being actually in commerce with mind via some mode of mental activity or other, for example, being imagined, desired, believed, and so on. (This, however, is the doctrine in *The Idea of Phenomenology*. Later on, when Husserl became preoccupied with transcendental subjectivity, which I shall mention below, he moved from this Platonic realism to a form of subjective idealism.)

The pure datum, the one to be located by the properly refined Cartesian method of doubt, is the immanent thing, in the "critical" sense of "immanent." To get to it, we need to go through several steps, each of which will be a refinement of Descartes's method of doubt. First, we need phenomenological reduction. This means suspending all beliefs characteristic of the "natural attitude," the attitude of common sense and science; in short, everything that is not "apodictic." Our perception of a chair, for instance, involves the belief that a physical chair is present "out there." This belief is neither necessarily true nor necessarily false. In the phenomenologically reduced state of the given, we are to hold in abeyance every such belief. And the same for mathematical objects. When we want to take a phenomenological look at say the number two, we are not to include in our thought of it that the number two has an objective, extramental though not physical, existence. The ἐποχή, the exclusion of transcendencies posited by the "natural attitude," is the first step of phenomenological analysis.

The second step is to perform an *eidetic reduction*, whereby in the particular occasion of say the perception of a chair, we bring ourselves to grasp perception as a universal; we make the pure essence of perception give itself to our pure intuition. The universals that become objects of phenomenological investigation cannot be had except through actual experience. A blind man, for instance, could never "get at" the essence of seeing because he cannot see. The phenomenologist must be in a position to "take a look" at what is going on when he is actually seeing something. Only then can he describe what seeing is as such as against *this* occasion of his seeing *that* object. What is more, phenomenological description is, as of old, not interested in causal or genetic accounts about the conditions under which the universals "give themselves" to pure intuition.

The third step is to discern the manner in which objects of cognition are *constituted* in cognition. This, says Husserl, requires much more than simply "looking" at the reduced phenomena. It requires a very careful scrutiny of the manner in which, within cognition, objects are compounded or synthesized according to stable regularities that are not psychological laws of association but are rather the forms of cognitive acts. For example, Husserl takes up sound as a phenomenon and suggests that the momentarily perceived tone is distinct from sound as a phenomenon. Sound is perceived as having time-phases, yet the phases are not given at any moment. They are formally constitutive of what sound is essentially (which is to be distinguished from sound as described in physics).

To put it in a simple and summary fashion, the phenomenologist is in search of a "pure" or "reduced" object, the essence of a special thing or of a process, such as seeing. He supposes that the process is unclear and indistinct in its everyday context. In the case of seeing, the "pure" or "reduced" phenomenon would be *seeing* plus a *cogitatio*, an act of attention focused upon seeing, to find out what seeing *is*. In the natural, everyday context, there is simply seeing. Wittgenstein, in his *Philosophical Investigations*,[1] makes certain devastating observations against the phenomenological program. For instance, *seeing* plus an effort to find out what seeing *is* is different from seeing as it ordinarily occurs. But the reader should read the above-mentioned references for the rewarding details.

In *The Idea of Phenomenology* Husserl hints at a doctrine that was later to become very important in his thought — the centrality of the transcendental ego. In the fourteenth edition of the *Encyclopaedia Britannica* Husserl has an article on Phenomenology. In it he describes transcendental subjectivity as follows:

Psychical subjectivity, the "I" and "we" of everyday intent, may be as it is in itself under the phenomenological-psychological reduction, and being eidetically treated, may establish a phenomenological psychology. But the transcendental subjectivity which for want of language we can

[1] Ludwig Wittgenstein, *Philosophical Investigations*, Oxford, Blackwell, 1953. Cf. Part I, Sections 153, 165–172, 202, 232. See also Paul Feyerabend, "Wittgenstein's Philosophical Investigations," *Philosophical Revue*, LXIV (July, 1955), esp. 456–460.

only call again, "I myself," "we ourselves," cannot be found under the attitude of psychological or natural science, being no part at all of the objective world, but that subjective conscious life itself, wherein the world and all its content is made for "us," for "me." We that are, indeed, men, spiritual and bodily, existing in the world, are, therefore, "appearances" unto ourselves, parcel of what "we" have constituted, pieces of the significance "we" have made. The "I" and the "we," which apprehend, presuppose the hidden "I" and "we" to whom they are "present."

Transcendental subjectivity, Husserl continues, requires a further reduction, the transcendental reduction. In this we not only hold in abeyance the things and features of things we posit through the "natural attitude" (cf. Santayana's "animal faith") but also "bracket out" the phenomenal selves, including our own self. The idea is to reduce the whole of reality to transcendentally reduced data. Otherwise put, the idea is to construct the whole reality from transcendentally reduced data. This is his way of taking up Descartes's problem about the reality of "the external world," the world of bodies and other minds. The philosophical motivation, one may safely suppose, is the one common to all forms of subjective idealism. It is to avoid the paradox Berkeley saw in Descartes.

Husserl's theory of transcendental subjectivity is not original with him. He is cognizant of the sorts of considerations that Hume and Kant were trying to take account of. Hume said: "... when I enter most intimately into what I call *myself*, I always stumble on some particular perception or other, of heat or cold, light or shade, love or hatred, pain or pleasure. I never catch *myself* at any time without a perception, and never can observe anything but the perception." Consistent with his brand of empiricism, Hume took this correct observation to imply that there is no such thing as a self. But his denial is paradoxical at least in the sense that the denial presupposes the existence of that which is being denied. Kant came to the opposite conclusion from Hume. We have to admit the reality of the transcendental self, said Kant, and Husserl follows Kant in this.

Thus, having been an antipsychologistic "realist" in the *Logical Investigations*, and having passed through a period of Platonic realism, Husserl ended as a radical subjectivist. For transcendental subjectivity led Husserl to a sort of subjective idealism. Husserl thought of his "transcendental-phenomenological idealism" as a strictly demonstrable position. He seems to have reasoned as follows: "The world" cannot be thought of except as being "constituted" by the transcendental ego's intentional acts. It follows, says Husserl, that nothing can exist if it is not dependent for its existence on the transcendental self. This implies that the essences emerging as residues at the end of phenomenological and transcendental reduction as well as bodies and other minds are existentially dependent upon the transcendental ego.

This sort of inference is characteristic of subjective idealism, and it is obviously invalid without further supplementation. There is an ambiguity in the phrase "being constituted." If it means *being brought into existence*, the premise is a patent falsehood. Many people think of "the world" as existing before there were any transcendental selves. Husserl needs a correct argument, nowhere given by him or any subjective idealist, to prove that to think this is logically inconsistent. If, however, the phrase "being constituted" means *being knowable*, then from the tautology that to be thought of as knowable is to be thought of as being capable of being accessible to a knower, it does not follow that nothing can exist if it is not dependent for its existence on the transcendental self. So far, then, Husserl has not created a "scientific" and unassailable "phenomenological idealism." Husserl carries his argument further. He says that the transcendental self itself is not existentially dependent upon anything else; and, therefore, the only real absolute is the transcendental ego, all else being existentially dependent on it (relative to it). But the final conclusion that the real absolute is transcendental subjectivity does not follow from the argument. For we have not been shown that everything else in the world is existentially dependent upon the transcendental self. The final phase of Husserl's philosophy is thus subject to the standard criticisms against classical forms of subjective idealism.

There are basic difficulties in the philosophical method Husserl preaches. One is his ultimate reliance on intuiting essences. This erects needless barriers to fruitful philosophical communication. Whenever Husserl asks us to take an intuitive "look" at some object, say "seeing as such," many a philosopher would be stymied. It has been suggested that "Husserl's fundamental contributions are much simpler than they at first appear to be. Thus there is little more to his transcendental ἐποχή and examination of essences than a determination to examine the meaning of common concepts and ordinary beliefs rather than to add factual detail to our knowledge. His program is, in fact, not very different from that of modern British and United States analytic philosophy." [1] There is some truth in these remarks. Husserl's detailed and valuable analyses of perceiving, believing, valuing, feeling, consciousness, and evidence in the early *Logische Untersuchungen* and the later *Ideen zu einer reinen Phänomenologie und phänomenologischen Philosophie* [2] may, without distortion, be taken as making conceptual points, that is, points about the logic of discourse. Thus, in *practice*, a good deal of Husserl's work is not unlike that of English-speaking analysts. But Husserl's *theory* of philosophical method, the phenomenological method, with its ultimate reliance on intuiting the essence of this or that entity is radically different from what philosophical method is conceived to be by many British or United States philosophers.

The phenomenological method with its ultimate appeal to intuition, not to the logic of language, makes *argument* impossible. As a way of *proving* anything, it is simply inadequate. In this connection it is worth recalling the remarks made earlier about Husserl's attack on psychologism in the *Logische Untersuchungen*. His appeals to intuiting necessary connections among abstract entities such as essences and propositions are weak in comparison with the argument that psychologism is viciously circular. *That* argument is not connected with the phenomenological attitude as such.

Husserl's *theory* of philosophical method involves two further and related difficulties. First, it is rather uncritical of Husserl to assume that there are, independently of any linguistic context, objects that are epistemologically absolute data. This is the Husserlian counterpart of logical atomism's assumption of ultimate absolute simples out of which "the world" is to be "logically

[1] See J. N. Findlay's article on phenomenology in *Encyclopaedia Britannica*, London, 1959, 14th edition.

[2] An English transcription of the *Logische Untersuchungen*, together with a discussion of Husserl's ideas, form the bulk of Marvin Farber's *The Foundations of Phenomenology* (see note 2, p. XII). This is a basic source book on Husserl. A more recent and equally basic source book is Farber's *Naturalism and Subjectivism*, Springfield, Ill., Charles C. Thomas, 1959.

constructed." The generic view that there are absolute rock-bottom elements has been powerfully criticized in the recent literature, for example, in Wittgenstein's *Philosophical Investigations*. Second, the shifting of the burden away from language and upon the self-evidently given indicates a somewhat naive view of the role of language: "we can make our speech conform in a pure measure to what is intuited in its full clarity," writes Husserl, (Lecture II, p. 24, *The Idea of Phenomenology*) as if language were the sort of thing that the phenomenologist could create at will in the image of ultimate facts.

That Husserl's work should be controversial and not altogether lucid is not an anomaly in philosophy. But it is no less philosophically interesting for these reasons. Moreover, his work has exerted an enormous influence on major philosophical movements current in Latin-America and Western Europe.

Indirectly phenomenology has also given direction to some European psychologists, for example, Binswanger and Buytendijk. So that anyone who hopes to achieve a comprehensive view of the contemporary philosophical scene needs to study Husserl.[1]

G. N.

---

[1] I wish to thank Prof. R. M. Chisholm for letting me see, prior to publication, his introduction to *Realism and the Background of Phenomenology* (see note 1, p. XIV).

THE IDEA OF PHENOMENOLOGY

Natural thinking in science and everyday life is untroubled by the difficulties concerning the possibility of cognition. *Philosophical thinking* is circumscribed by one's position toward the problems concerning the possibility of cognition. The perplexities in which reflection about the possibility of a cognition that "gets at" the things themselves becomes entangled: How can we be sure that cognition accords with things as they exist in themselves, that it "gets at them"? What do things in themselves care about our ways of thinking and the logical rules governing them? These are laws of how we think; they are psychological laws — Biologism, psychological laws as laws of adaptation.

Absurdity: to begin with, when we think naturally about cognition and fit it and its achievements into the natural ways of thinking which pertains to the sciences we arrive at theories that are appealing at first. But they end in contradiction or absurdity — Inclination to open scepticism.

Even this attempt to look at these problems scientifically we can call "theory of knowledge." At any rate what emerges is the idea of a theory of knowledge as a science which solves the above-mentioned difficulties, gives us an ultimate, clear, therefore inherently consistent insight into the essence of cognition and the possibility of its achievements. The critique of cognition in this sense is the condition of the possibility of a metaphysics.

The *method* of the critique of cognition is the phenomenological method, phenomenology as the general doctrine of essences, within which the science of the essence of cognition finds its place.

What sort of method is this? How can a science of cognition be established if cognition in general, what cognizing means and can accomplish, is questioned? What method can here reach the goal?

<4> A. The First Step in the Phenomenological Orien-
tation

1) Right away we become dubious whether such a science is at
all possible. If it questions all cognition, every cognition chosen as
a starting point is questioned. How then can it ever begin?

This, however, is only a specious difficulty. In "being called
into question," cognition is neither *disavowed* nor regarded as in
every sense doubtful. The question is about some accomplish-
ments imputed to cognition, whereas in fact it is even an open
question whether the difficulties pertain to all possible types of
cognition. At any rate, if the theory of knowledge is to concern itself with the possibility of cognition it must have cognitions of
the possibilities of cognition which, as such, are beyond question;
indeed, cognitions in the fullest sense, cognitions about which
absolutely no doubt of their having reached their objects is
possible. If we are uncertain or unclear as to how it is possible
for cognition to reach its object, and if we are inclined to doubt
that such a thing is possible, we must, first of all, have before us
indubitable examples of cognitions or possible cognitions which
really reach, or would reach, their respective objects. At the outset we must not take anything as a cognition just because it
seems to be one; otherwise we would have no possible, or what
comes to the same thing, no sensible objective.

Here the *Cartesian method of doubt* provides a starting point.
Without doubt there is *cogitatio*, there is, namely, the mental
process during the [subject's] undergoing it and in a simple
reflection upon it. The seeing, direct grasping and having of the
cogitatio is already a cognition. The *cogitationes* are the first
absolute data.   acts of consciousness

2) What follows naturally is our *first question in the theory of
knowledge:* What distinguishes the certainty in these examples
from the uncertainty in other instances of alleged cognition? Why
is there in certain cases a tendency toward scepticism and toward
asking the sceptical question: How can cognition reach a being,
and why is there not this doubt and this difficulty in connection
with the *cogitationes?*

<5>   People answer at first — that is indeed the answer ready at
hand — in terms of the pair of concepts or words *immanence* and
transcendence. The "seeing" cognition of the *cogitatio* is immanent.

The cognition belonging to the objective sciences, the natural sciences and the sciences of culture (*Geisteswissenschaften*) and on closer inspection also the mathematical sciences, is transcendent. Involved in the objective sciences is the *doubtfulness of transcendence*, the question: How can cognition reach beyond itself? How can it reach a being that is not to be found within the confines of consciousness? There is not this difficulty with the "seeing" cognition of the *cogitatio*.[1]

3) Next, one is inclined to interpret, as if this were obvious, immanence as genuine immanence (*reelle Immanenz*) [2] and even perhaps to interpret it psychologically, as *immanence in something real (reale Immanenz)*: the object of cognition too, is within the cognitive process as a real actuality, or in the [stream of] ego-consciousness of which the mental process is a part. That the cognitive act can hit upon and find its object in the same [stream of] consciousness and within the same real here and now, that is what is taken for granted. The neophyte will say, at this point, that the immanent is in me, the transcendent outside of me.

On a closer view, however, *genuine immanence (reelle Immanenz)* differs from *immanence in the sense of self-givenness as constituted in evidence (Evidenz)*. The genuinely immanent (*reell Immanente*) is taken as the indubitable just on account of the fact that it presents nothing else, "points" to nothing "outside" itself, for what is here intended is fully and adequately given in itself. Any self-givenness other than that of the genuinely immanent (*reell Immanente*) is not yet in view.

4) So for the moment no distinction is made. The first step toward clarity now is this: the genuinely immanent (*reell Immanentes*), or what would here mean the same, the adequately self-given, is beyond question. I may make use of it. That which is transcendent (not genuinely immanent) I may not use. Therefore,

---

[1] Tr. note: we have rendered Husserl's word *schauen* as "see," the point of the double quotes being that this use of "see" is broader than simply seeing with one's eyes.

[2] Tr. note: *reelle Immanenz* has no straightforward translation. The distinction Husserl has in mind is the immanence of universals (essences) vs. the (*reelle*) immanence of mental occurrences and their *contents*, *e.g.*, *cogitationes*, their contents; also, psychological occurrences such as toothaches. Everything (*reell*) immanent is existentially mind-dependent. Essences, on the other hand, are neither mental *occurrences* nor *contents*. They are intentionally inexistent *objects* of cognitive acts, specifically of "seeings," but they are not ingredients of such acts. Their immanence is simply their *givenness* to "seeing."

I must accomplish a *phenomenological reduction: I must exclude all that is transcendently posited.*

Why? [Because] if I am in the dark as to how cognition can reach that which is transcendent, not given in itself but "intended ‹6› as being outside," / no cognition or science of the transcendent can help to dispel the darkness. What I want is *clarity.* I want to understand *the possibility* of that reaching. But this, if we examine its sense, signifies: I want to come face to face with the essence of the possibility of that reaching. I want to make it given to me in an act of "seeing." A "seeing" cannot be demonstrated. The blind man who wishes to see cannot be made to see by means of scientific proofs. Physical and physiological theories about colors give no "seeing" (*schauende*) clarity about the meaning of color as those with eyesight have it. If, therefore, the critique of cognition is a science, as it doubtless is in the light of these considerations, a science which is to clarify all species and forms of cognition, *it can make no use of any science of the natural sort.* It cannot tie itself to the conclusions that any natural science has reached about what is. For it they remain in question. As far as the critique of cognition is concerned, all the sciences are only *phenomena of science.* Every tie of that sort signifies a defective μετάβασις (foundation). This comes about only by way of a mistaken but often seductive *shifting between problems:* between explaining cognition as a fact of nature in psychological and scientific terms and elucidating cognition in terms of its essential capabilities to accomplish its task. Accordingly, if we are to avoid this confusion and remain constantly mindful of the meaning of the question concerning these capabilities, we need *phenomenological reduction.*

This means: everything transcendent (that which is not given to me immanently) is to be assigned the index zero, i.e., its existence, its validity is not to be assumed as such, except at most as *the phenomenon of a claim to validity.* I am to treat all sciences only as phenomena, hence not as systems of valid truths, not as premises, not even as hypotheses for me to reach truth with. This applies to the whole of psychology and the whole of natural science. Meanwhile, the proper *meaning of our principle* is in the constant challenge to stay with the objects as they are in question *here* in the critique of cognition and not to confuse the problems *here* with quite different ones. The elucidation of the ways in which cognition is possible does not depend upon the ways of objective science. / To bring knowledge to evident self-givenness ‹7› and to seek to view the nature of its accomplishment does not mean to deduce, to make inductions, to calculate, etc. It is not the same as eliciting, with reasons, novel things from things already given or purportedly given.

B. The Second Level of the Phenomenological Orientation

We now need a *new stratum of considerations* in order to achieve a higher level of clarity about the nature of phenomenological research and its problems.

1) First, the Cartesian *cogitatio* already requires the phenomenological reduction. The psychological phenomenon in psychological apperception and objectification is not a truly absolute datum. The truly absolute datum is the *pure phenomenon*, that which is reduced. The mentally active ego, the object, man in time, the thing among things, etc., are not absolute data; hence man's mental activity as his activity is no absolute datum either. *We abandon finally the standpoint of psychology, even of descriptive psychology.* And so what is also *reduced* is the question which initially drove us: no longer how can I, this man, contact in my mental processes something existing in itself, perhaps out there, beyond me; but we now replace this hitherto ambiguous question, unstable and complex, because of its transcendent burden, with the *pure basic question:* How can the pure phenomenon of cognition reach something which is not immanent to it? How can the absolute self-givenness of cognition reach something not self-given and how is this reaching to be understood?

At the same time the concept of *genuine immanence* (*reellen Immanenz*) is reduced. It no longer signifies immanence in something *real* (*reale Immanenz*), the immanence in human consciousness and in the real (*realen*) psychic phenomenon.

2) Once we have the "seen" phenomena, it seems that we already have a phenomenology, a science of these phenomena.

But as soon as we begin there, we notice a certain constriction. / ‹8› The field of absolute phenomena — taken one at a time — does not seem to be enough to fulfill our intentions. What good are single "seeings" to us, no matter how securely they bring our *cogitationes* to self-givenness? At first it seems beyond question that on the basis of these "seeings" we can undertake logical operations, can compare, contrast, subsume under concepts, predicate, although, as appears later, behind these operations stand new objectivities. But even if what here seems beyond question were taken for granted and considered no further, we could not understand how we could here arrive at universally valid findings of the sort we need.

But one thing seems to help us along: *eidetic abstraction*. It yields inspectable universals, species, essences, and so it seems to provide the redeeming idea: for do we not seek "seeing" clarity about the essence of cognition? Cognition belongs to the sphere of *cogitationes*. Accordingly, we must through "seeing" bring its universal objects into the consciousness of the universal. Thus it becomes possible to have a doctrine about the essence of cognition.

We take this step in agreement with a tenet of Descartes's concerning *clear and distinct perceptions*. The "existence" of the *cogitatio* is guaranteed by its absolute *self-givenness*, by its givenness in *pure evidence* (*Evidenz*). Whenever we have pure evidence (*Evidenz*), the pure viewing and grasping of something objective directly and in itself, we have the same guarantees, the same certainties.

This step gave us a new objectivity as absolutely given, i.e., the *objectivity of essences;* and as to begin with the logical acts which find expression in assertions based upon what is intuited remain unnoticed, so now we get the field of *assertions about essences*, viz., of what is generally the case as given in pure "seeing." That is to say at first undifferentiated from the individually given universal objects.

3) Yet do we now have everything; do we have the fully delineated phenomenology and the clear self-evidence to put us in the position of having what we need for the critique of cog-
‹9› nition? / And are we clear about the issues to be resolved?

No, the step we took leads us further. It makes clear to us in the first place that *genuine (reell) immanence* (and the same is true of transcendence) is but a special case of the *broader concept of immanence as such*. No longer is it a commonplace and taken on face value that *the absolutely given* and the *genuinely immanent* are one and the same. For that which is universal is absolutely given but is not genuinely immanent. *The act of cognizing* the universal is something singular. At any given time, it is a moment in the stream of consciousness. *The universal itself*, which is given in evidence (*Evidenz*) within the stream of consciousness is nothing singular but just a universal, and in the genuine (*reellen*) sense it is transcendent.

Consequently, the idea of *phenomenological reduction* acquires a more immediate and more profound determination and a clearer meaning. It means not the exclusion of the genuinely transcendent (perhaps even in some psychologico-empirical sense), but the exclusion of the transcendent as such as something to be accepted as existent, i.e., everything that is not evident givenness in its true sense, that is not absolutely given to pure "seeing." But, of course, everything of what we said remains. Inductive or deductive scientific conclusions or facets, etc., from hypotheses, facts, axioms, remain excluded and are allowed only as "phenomena"; and the same with all reference to any "knowing" and "cognition": inquiry must concern itself always with *pure "seeing"* and, therefore, not with the genuinely immanent. It is inquiry within the sphere of pure evidence, inquiry into essences. We also said that its field is the *a priori within absolute self-givenness*.

Thus the field is now characterized. It is a field of absolute cognitions, within which the ego and the world and God and the mathematical manifolds and whatever else may be a scientifically objective matter are held in abeyance, cognitions which are, therefore, also not dependent on these matters, which are valid in their own right, whether we are sceptics with regard to the others or not. All that remains as it is. The root of the matter, however, is *to grasp the meaning of the absolutely given, the absolute clarity of the given*, which / excludes every meaningful doubt, in a <10> word, *to grasp the absolutely "seeing" evidence which gets hold of itself*. To a certain extent in the discovery of all this lies the historical significance of the Cartesian method of doubt. But for Descartes to discover and to abandon were the same. We do nothing but clearly formulate and develop consistently what was always implicit in this age-old project. We part company in this connection with psychologistic interpretations of evidence in terms of feelings.

C. The Third Level of the Phenomenological Orientation

Once more we need a new level of considerations, to give us greater clarity about the meaning of phenomenology and to develop further its problems.

How far does self-givenness reach? Is it contained in the givenness of the *cogitatio* and in the ideations which grasp it in its generality? Our phenomenological sphere, the sphere of absolute clarity, of immanence in the true sense, reaches no farther than self-givenness reaches.

We are once again led somewhat deeper, and in depths lie the obscurities and in the obscurities lie the problems.

Everything seemed at first simple and hardly requiring hard work. The prejudice about immanence as genuine immanence, as if the latter were what mattered, one may cast off, and yet one remains at first wedded to genuine immanence, at least in a certain sense. It seems, at first, that in "seeing" essences we have only to grasp in its generality the genuinely immanent in the *cogitationes* and to establish the connections rooted in essences. This, too, seems an easy matter. We reflect; we look back at our own acts; we appraise their genuine contents, as they are, only under phenomenological reduction. This appears to be the sole difficulty. And now, of course, there is nothing further than to lift that which is "seen" into consciousness of universality.

The matter, however, becomes less cozy when we take a closer <11> look at the data. First, the *cogitationes*, which / we regard as simple data and in no way mysterious, hide all sorts of transcendencies.

If we look closer and notice how in the mental process, say of [perceiving] a sound, even after phenomenological reduction, *appearance and that which appears stand in contrast*, and this *in the midst of pure givenness*, hence in the midst of true immanence, then we are taken aback. Perhaps the sound lasts. We have there the patently given unity of the sound and its duration with its temporal phases, the present and the past. On the other hand, when we reflect, the phenomenon of enduring sound, itself a temporal phenomenon, has its own now-phase and past phases. And if one picks out a now-phase of the phenomenon there is not only the objective now of the sound itself, but the now of the sound is but a point in the duration of a sound.

Detailed analyses will be given in the course of our special tasks. The above suggestion is enough to call attention to a new point: that the phenomenon of sound perception, even as evident and reduced, demands within the immanent a distinction between *appearance* and *that which appears*. We thus have two absolute data, the givenness of the appearing and the givenness of the object; and the object within this immanence is not immanent in the sense of genuine immanence; it is not a concrete part (*Stück*) of the appearance, i.e., the past phases of the enduring sound are now still objective and yet they are not genuinely contained in the present moment of the appearance. Therefore, we also find in the case of the phenomenon of perception what we found in the case of consciousness of universals, namely, that it is a consciousness which constitutes something self-given which is not contained within what is occurring [in the world] and is not at all found as *cogitatio*.

At the lowest level of reflection, the naive level, at first it seems as if evidence were a matter of simple "seeing," a mental inspection without a character of its own, always one and the same and in itself undifferentiated: the "seeing" just "sees" the things (*Sachen*), / the things are simply there and in the truly ‹12› evident "seeing" they are there in consciousness, and "seeing" is simply to "see" them. Or, to use our previous simile: a direct grasping or taking or pointing to something that simply is and is there. All difference is thus in the things that exist in themselves and have their differences through themselves.

And now how different the "seeing" of things shows itself to be on closer analysis. Even if we retain under the heading of attention the notion of an undifferentiated and in itself no further describable "seeing," it is, nevertheless, apparent that it really makes no sense at all to talk about things which are "simply there" and just need to be "seen." On the contrary, this "simply being there" consists of certain mental processes of specific and changing structure, such as perception, imagination, memory, predication, etc., and in them the things are not contained as in a hull or vessel. Instead, the things come to be *constituted* in these mental processes, although in reality they are

not at all to be found in them. For "things to be given" is for
them to be *exhibited* (represented) as so and so in such phenomena.
And this is not to say that the things once more exist in themselves and "send their representatives into consciousness." This
sort of thing cannot occur to us within the sphere of phenomenological reduction. Instead, the things are and are given in appearance and in virtue of the appearance itself; though they are,
or are taken as, individually separable from the appearance, they
are essentially inseparable from it insofar as the single appearance (the consciousness of the given) is not in question.

Thus this marvelous correlation between the *phenomenon of
cognition* and the *object of cognition* reveals itself everywhere.
Now let us notice that the task of phenomenology, or rather the
area of its tasks and inquiries, is no such trivial things as merely
looking, merely opening one's eyes. Already in the first and
simplest cases, in the lowest forms of cognition, the greatest
difficulties confront pure analysis and the inspection of essences.
It is easy to talk of correlation in general but it is very difficult
to clarify the way in which an object of cognition *constitutes* itself
<13> in cognition. / And the task is just this: within the framework of
pure evidence (*Evidenz*) or self-givenness *to trace all forms of
givenness and all correlations* and to conduct an elucidatory
analysis. Of course, to do this we need to take account not only of
single acts but also of their complexities, of the consistency or
inconsistency of their connections and of the intentions (*Teleo-
logien*) apparent in them. These connections are not conglo-
merations but distinctively connected and as it were congruent
unities, and unities of cognition, which, as unities of cognition
have also their unitary objective correlates. Thus they belong
themselves to the *cognitive acts*, their types are cognitive types,
their native forms are forms of thought and forms of intuition
(the word not here to be taken in its Kantian sense).

It now remains to trace step by step the data in all their
modifications, those that are, properly speaking, data and those
that are not, the simple and the compounded ones, those that so
to say are constituted at once and those that essentially are built
up stepwise, those that are absolutely valid and those that in the
process of cognition acquire givenness and validity in an un-
limited progression.

We finally arrive in this way at an understanding of how the transcendent real object can be met (can be known in its nature) in the cognitive act as that which one primarily means by it, and how the sense of this meaning is filled out step by step in a developing cognitive context (if only it has the proper forms which belong to the constitution of the object of experience). We then understand how the object of experience is progressively constituted, and how this manner of being constituted is prescribed. We understand that such a stepwise constitution is required by the very essence of the experienced object.

Along this path one approaches the methodological forms which determine all the sciences and are constitutive of all scientifically given objects, and so also the elucidation of the theory of science and with it implicitly the elucidation of all the sciences; however, only implicitly, i.e., it is only once this enormous work of elucidation has been accomplished that the critique of cognition will be fit to become / a critique of the ‹14› specialized sciences and thereby to evaluate them metaphysically.

These then are the problems of givenness, the problems of the *constitution of objects of all sorts within cognition*. The phenomenology of cognition is the science of cognitive phenomena in two senses. On the one hand it has to do with cognitions as appearances, presentations, acts of consciousness in which this or that object is presented, is an object of consciousness, passively or actively. On the other hand, the phenomenology of cognition has to do with these objects as presenting themselves in this manner. The word "phenomenon" is ambiguous in virtue of the essential correlation between *appearance and that which appears*. Φαινόμενον (phenomenon) in its proper sense means that which appears, and yet it is by preference used for the appearing itself, for the subjective phenomenon (if one may use this expression which is apt to be misunderstood in the vulgar psychological sense).

In reflection, the *cogitatio*, the appearing itself, becomes an object, and this encourages the rise of ambiguity. Finally, we need not repeat once more that in speaking about investigating the objects and modes of cognition, we always mean investigation into essences, which, in the sphere of the absolutely given, exhibits in a general way the ultimate meaning, the possibility, the essence of the objectivity of cognition and of the cognition of objects.

It goes without saying that the *general phenomenology of reason* has to solve also the parallel problems of the correlation between *valuing* and the *things valued*, etc. If the word "phenomenology" were used so broadly as to cover the analysis of everything self-given, the incoherent data would become coherent: analyzing sense-given entities according to their various kinds, etc. — the common element is then in the methodology of the analysis of essences within the sphere of immediate evidence.

In earlier lectures I distinguished between *science of the natural* ‹17› *sort* and *philosophic science*. The former originates from the natural, the latter from the philosophic attitude of mind.

The *natural attitude of mind* is as yet unconcerned with the critique of cognition. Whether in the act of intuiting or in the act of thinking, in the natural mode of reflection we are turned to *the objects* as they are given to us each time and as a matter of course, even though they are given in different ways and in different modes of being, according to the source and level of our cognition. In perception, for instance, a thing stands before our eyes as a matter of course. It is there, among other things, living or lifeless, animate or inanimate. It is, in short, within a world of which part is perceived, as are the individual things themselves, and of which part is contextually supplied by memory from whence it spreads out into the indeterminate and the unknown.

Our judgments relate to this world. We make (sometimes singular, sometimes universal) judgments about things, their relations, their changes, about the conditions which functionally determine their changes and about the laws of their variations. We find an expression for what immediate experience presents. en line with our experiential motives we draw inferences from the Iirectly experienced (perceived and remembered) to what is not dxperienced. We generalize, and then apply again general knowledge to particular cases or deduce analytically new generalizations from general knowledge. Isolated cognitions do not simply follow each other in the manner of mere succession. They enter into logical relations with each other, they follow from one another, they "cohere" with one another, they support one another, thereby strengthening their logical power.

On the other hand, they also clash and contradict one another. They do not agree with one another, they are falsified by *assured* cognition, / and their claim to be cognition is discredited. Perhaps the contradictions arise in the sphere that belongs to laws governing the pure predicational form: we have equivocated, we have inferred fallaciously, we have miscounted or mis-computed. In these cases we restore formal consistency. We resolve the equivocation and the like.

Or the contradictions disturb our expectation of connections based on past experience: empirical evidence conflicts with empirical evidence. Where do we look for help? We now weigh the reasons for different possible ways of deciding or providing an explanation. The weaker must give way to the stronger, and the stronger, in turn, are of value as long as they will stand up, i.e., as long as they in turn do not have to come into a similar logical conflict with new cognitional motives introduced by a broader sphere of cognition.

Thus, natural knowledge makes strides. It progressively takes possession of a reality at first existing for us as a matter of course and as something to be investigated further as regards its extent and content, its elements, its relations and laws. Thus the various sciences of the natural sort (*natürlichen Wissenschaften*) come into being and flourish, the natural sciences (*Naturwissen-schaften*) as the sciences of physics and psychology, the sciences of culture (*Geisteswissenschaften*) and, on the other side, the mathematical sciences, the sciences of numbers, classes, relations, etc. The latter sciences deal not with actual but rather with ideal objects; they deal with what is valid *per se*, and for the rest with what are from the first unquestionable possibilities.

In every step of natural cognition pertaining to the sciences of the natural sort, difficulties arise and are resolved, either by *pure logic* or by appeal to *facts*, on the basis of motives or reasons which lie in the things themselves and which, as it were, come from things in the form of *requirements* that they themselves make on our thinking.

Now let us contrast the natural *mode* (*or habit*) of *reflection* with the *philosophical*.

With the awakening of reflection about the relation of cogni-tion to its object, abysmal difficulties arise. / Cognition, the thing most taken for granted in natural thinking, suddenly emerges as a mystery. But I must be more exact. What is *taken for granted* in natural thinking is the possibility of cognition. Constantly busy producing results, advancing from discovery to discovery in newer and newer branches of science, natural thinking finds no occasion to raise the question of the possibility of cognition as such. To be sure, as with everything else in the world, *cognition*, too, will appear as a problem in a *certain manner*, becoming an object of natural investigation. Cognition is a fact in nature. It is the experience of a cognizing organic being. It is a psychological fact. As any psychological fact, it can be described according to its kinds and internal connections, and its genetic relations can be investigated. On the other hand cognition is essentially *cognition of what objectively is;* and it is cognition through the *meaning* which is intrinsic to it; by virtue of this meaning it is *related* to what objectively is. Natural thinking is also already active in this relating. It investigates in their *formal* generality the *a priori* connections of meanings and postulated meanings and the *a priori* principles which belong to objectivity *as such;* there comes into being a *pure grammar* and at higher stages a pure logic (a whole complex of disciplines owing to its different possible delimitations), and there arises once more a normative and practical logic in the form of an art of thinking, and, especially, of scientific thinking.

So far, we are still in the realm of *natural* thinking.

However, the correlation between cognition as mental process, its referent (*Bedeutung*) and what objectively is, which has just been touched upon in order to contrast the psychology of cognition with pure logic and ontology, is the source of the deepest and most difficult problems. Taken collectively, they are the problem of the possibility of cognition.

Cognition in all of its manifestations is a psychic act; it is the <20> cognition of a cognizing subject. The objects cognized stand over and against the cognition. But how can we be certain of the correspondence between cognition and the object cognized? How can knowledge transcend itself and reach its object reliably? The unproblematic manner in which the object of cognition is given to natural thought to be cognized now becomes an enigma. In perception the perceived thing is believed to be directly given. Before my perceiving eyes stands the thing. I see it, and I grasp it. Yet the perceiving is simply a mental act of mine, of the perceiving subject. Likewise, memory and expectation are subjective processes; and so are all thought processes built upon them and through which we come to posit that something really is the case and to determine any *truth* about what is. How do I, the cognizing subject, know if I can ever really know, that there exist not only my own mental processes, these acts of cognizing, but also that which they apprehend? How can I ever know that there is anything at all which could be set over against cognition as its object?

Shall I say: only phenomena are truly given to the cognizing subject, he never does and never can break out of the circle of his own mental processes, so that in truth he could only say: I exist, and all that is not-I is mere phenomenon dissolving into phenomenal connections? Am I then to become a solipsist? This is a hard requirement. Shall I, with Hume, reduce all transcendent objectivity to fictions lending themselves to psychological explanation but to no rational justification? But this, too, is a hard requirement. Does not Hume's psychology, along with any psychology, transcend the sphere of immanence? By working with such concepts as habit, human nature, sense-organ, stimulus and the like, is it not working with transcendent existences (and transcendent by its own avowal), while its aim is to degrade to the status of fictions everything that transcends actual "impressions" and "ideas"?

But what is the use of invoking the specter of contradictions
‹21› when / *logic itself is in question* and becomes problematic. *Indeed, the real meaning of logical lawfulness* which natural thinking would not dream of questioning, now becomes *problematic* and *dubious*. Thoughts of a biological order intrude. We are reminded of the modern theory of evolution, according to which man has evolved in the struggle for existence and by natural selection, and with him his intellect too has evolved naturally and along with his intellect all of its characteristic forms, particularly the logical forms. Accordingly, is it not the case that the logical forms and laws express the accidental peculiarity of the human species, which could have been different and which will be different in the course of future evolution? Cognition is, after all, only

human cognition, bound up with *human intellectual forms*, and unfit to reach the very nature of things, to reach the things in themselves.

But at once another piece of absurdity arises. Can the cognitions by which such a view operates and the possibilities which it ponders make any sense themselves if the laws of logic are given over to such relativism? Does not the truth that there is this and that possibility implicitly presuppose the absolute validity of the principle of non-contradiction, according to which any given truth excludes its contradictory?

These examples should suffice. The possibility of cognition has become enigmatic throughout. If we immerse ourselves in the sciences of the natural sort, we find everything clear and comprehensible, to the extent to which they have developed into exact sciences. We are certain that we are in possession of objective truth, based upon reliable methods of reaching (objective) reality. But whenever we reflect, we fall into errors and confusions. We become entangled in patent difficulties and even self-contradictions. We are in constant danger of becoming sceptics, or still worse, we are in danger of falling into any one of a number of scepticisms all of which have, sad to say, one and the same characteristic: absurdity.

The playground of these unclear and inconsistent theories as well as the endless quarrels associated with them / is the *theory* ‹22› *of knowledge*, and *metaphysics* which is bound up with it historically and in subject matter. The task of the theory of knowledge or the critique of theoretical reason is, first of all, a critical one. It must brand the well-nigh inevitable mistakes which ordinary reflection makes about the relation of cognition, its meaning and its object, thereby refuting the concealed as well as the unconcealed sceptical theories concerning the essence of cognition by demonstrating their absurdity.

Furthermore, the positive task of the theory of knowledge is to solve the problems of the relations among cognition, its meaning and its object by inquiring into the essence of cognition. Among these, there is the problem of explicating the essential meaning of being a cognizable object or, what comes to the same thing, of being an object at all: of the meaning which is prescribed (for being an object at all) by the correlation *a priori* (or essential correlation) between cognition and being an object of cognition. And this naturally applies also to all basic forms of being an object which are predetermined by the nature of cognition. (To the ontological, the apophantic [1] as well as the metaphysical forms.)

Precisely by solving these problems the theory of knowledge qualifies as the critique of cognition, more exactly, as *the critique of natural cognition* in all the sciences of a natural sort. It puts us, in other words, in a position to interpret in an accurate and definitive way the teachings of these sciences about what exists. For the confusions of the theory of knowledge into which we are led by natural (pre-epistemological) reflection on the possibility of cognition (on the possibility of cognition's reaching its object) involve not just false views about the essence of cognition, but also self-contradictory, and, therefore, fundamentally misleading *interpretations* of the being that is cognized in the sciences of the natural sort. So, one and the same science is interpreted in materialistic, spiritualistic, dualistic, psychomonistic, positivistic and many other ways, depending upon what interpretation is thought to be the necessary consequence of those pre-epistemological reflections. Only with epistemological reflection do we
‹23› arrive at the distinction between / the sciences of a natural sort and philosophy. Epistemological reflection first brings to light that the sciences of a natural sort are not yet the ultimate science of being. We need a science of being in the absolute sense. This science, which we call *metaphysics*, grows out of a "critique" of natural cognition in the individual sciences. It is based on what is learned in the general critique of cognition about the essence of cognition and what it is to be an object of cognition of one basic type or other, i.e., in accordance with the different fundamental correlations between cognizing and being an object of cognition.

If then we disregard any metaphysical purpose of the critique of cognition and confine ourselves purely to the task *of clarifying the essence of cognition and of being an object of cognition, then this will be phenomenology of cognition and of being an object of cognition* and will be the first and principal part of phenomenology as a whole.

Phenomenology: this denotes a science, a system of scientific

---

[1] Tr. note: In Husserl the **word "apophantic" refers to predicative judgments** or to the theory of such judgments.

disciplines. But it also and above all denotes a method and an attitude of mind, the specifically *philosophical attitude* of mind, the specifically *philosophical method*.

In contemporary philosophy, insofar as it claims to be a serious science, it has become almost a commonplace that there can be only one method for achieving cognition in all the sciences as well as in philosophy. This conviction accords wholly with the great philosophical traditions of the seventeenth century, which also thought that philosophy's salvation lay wholly in its taking as a model of method the exact sciences, and above all, mathematics and mathematical natural science. This putting philosophy methodologically on a par with the other sciences goes hand in hand with treating them alike with respect to subject matter. It is still the prevailing opinion that philosophy and, more specifically, ontology and the general theory of knowledge not only relate to all the other sciences, but also that they can be grounded upon the conclusions of those other sciences: / in the ‹24› same way in which sciences are built upon one another, and the conclusions of one of them can serve as premises for the others. I am reminded of the favorite ploy of basing the theory of knowledge on the psychology of cognition and biology. In our day, reactions against these fatal prejudices are multiplying. And prejudices they are.

In the sphere of ordinary inquiry one science can readily build upon another, and the one can serve the other as a model of method even though to a limited extent determined by the nature of the areas of inquiry in question. *But philosophy lies in a wholly new dimension.* It needs an *entirely new point of departure* and an entirely new method distinguishing it in principle from any "natural" science. This is why the logical procedures that give the sciences of a natural sort unity have a unitary character in principle in spite of the special methods which change from one science to another: while the methodological procedures of philosophy have by contrast and in principle a new unity. This is also why *pure* philosophy, within the whole of the critique of cognition and the "critical" disciplines generally, must disregard, and must refrain from using, the intellectual achievements of the sciences of a natural sort and of scientifically undisciplined natural wisdom and knowledge.

To anticipate, this doctrine, the grounds for which will be given in more detail in the sequel, is recommended by the following considerations.

In the sceptical mood which critical reflection about cognition necessarily begets (I mean the reflection that comes first, the one that comes before the scientific critique of cognition and which takes place on the natural level of thought) every science of the natural sort and every method characteristic of such a science ceases to count as something we properly possess. For cognition's reaching its object has become enigmatic and dubious as far as its meaning and possibility are concerned, and exact cognition becomes thereby no less enigmatic than inexact, <25> scientific knowledge no / less than the pre-scientific. The possibility of cognition becomes questionable, more precisely, how it can possibly reach an objectivity which, after all, is in itself whatever it is. Behind this lies the following: What is in question is what cognition can accomplish, the meaning of its claim to validity and correctness, the meaning of the distinction between valid real and merely apparent cognition; on the other hand, also the meaning of being an object which exists and exists as what it is whether it is cognized or not and which as an object is an object of possible cognition, in principle cognizable, even if in fact it has never been and never will be cognized, but is in principle perceptible, imaginable, determinable by predicates in a possible judgment, etc.

However, it is impossible to see how working with presuppositions which are taken from natural cognition, no matter how "exactly founded" they are in it, can help us to resolve the misgivings which arise in the critique of cognition, to find the answers to its problems. If the meaning and value of natural cognition *as such* together with *all* of its methodological presuppositions and all of its exact foundations have become problematic, then this strikes at every proposition which natural cognition presupposes in its starting-point and at every allegedly exact method of giving a foundation. Neither the most exact mathematics nor mathematical natural science has here the slightest advantage over any actual or alleged cognition through ordinary experience. It is then clear that there can be no such talk as that philosophy (which begins in the critique of cognition and which, whatever else it is, is rooted in the critique of cognition) has to model itself after the exact sciences methodologically (or even as regards subject matter!), or that it has to adopt as a standard their methodology, or that it is philosophy's task to implement and to complete the work done in the exact sciences according to a single method, in principle the same for all the sciences. In contradistinction to all natural cognition, philosophy lies, I repeat, within a *new dimension;* and what corresponds to this new dimension, even if, as the phrase suggests, it is essentially connected with the old dimensions, is a *new* and *radically new method* which / is set over against the "natural" method. He who denies <26> this has failed to understand entirely the whole of the level at which the characteristic problem of the critique of cognition lies, and with this he has failed to understand what philosophy really wants to do and should do, and what gives it its own character and authority *vis-à-vis* the whole of natural cognition and science of the natural sort.

<27>

LECTURE II

<29> At the outset of the critique of cognition the entire world of
nature, physical and psychological, as well as one's own human
self together with all the sciences which have to do with these
objective matters, are *put in question*. Their being, their validity
are left up in the air.

Now the question is: How can *the critique of cognition get under
way?* The critique of cognition is the attempt of cognition to find
a scientific understanding of itself and to establish objectively
what cognition is in its essence, what is the meaning of the relation to an object which is implicit in the claim to cognition and
what its objective validity or the reaching of its object comes to
if it is to be cognition in the true sense. Although the ἐποχή,[1]
which the critique of cognition must employ, begins with the
doubt of all cognition, its own included, it cannot remain in such
doubt nor can it refuse to take as valid everything given, including that which it brings to light itself. If it must presuppose
nothing as *already given*, then it must begin with some cognition
which it does not take unexamined from elsewhere but rather
gives to itself, which it itself posits as primal.

This primal cognition must contain nothing of the unclarity
and the doubt which otherwise give to cognition the character of
the enigmatic and problematic so that we are finally in the
embarrassing position of having to say that cognition as such is a
problem, something incomprehensible, in need of elucidation
and dubious in its claims. Or, to speak differently: If we are not
allowed to take anything as already given because our lack of
clarity about cognition implies that we cannot understand what

---

[1] Tr. note: *epoche*, the excluding of transcendencies posited by the "natural
attitude."

it could mean for something *to be known in itself* yet *in the context of cognition*, then it must after all be possible to make evident something which we have to acknowledge as absolutely given and indubitable; / insofar, that is, as it is given with such complete ‹30› clarity that every question about it will and must find an immediate answer.

And now we recall the Cartesian doubt. Reflecting on the multifarious possibilities of error and deception, I might reach such a degree of sceptical despair that I finally say: Nothing is certain, everything is doubtful. But it is at once evident that not everything is doubtful, for while I am judging that everything is doubtful, it is indubitable that I am so judging; and it would be absurd to want to persist in a universal doubt. And in every case of a definite doubt, it is indubitably certain that I have this doubt. And likewise with every *cogitatio*. Howsoever I perceive, imagine, judge, infer, howsoever these acts may be certain or uncertain, whether or not they have objects that exist as far as the perceiving itself is concerned, it is absolutely clear and certain that I am perceiving this or that, and as far as the judgment is concerned that I am judging of this or that, etc.

Descartes introduced these considerations for other purposes. But with suitable modifications, we can use them here.

If we inquire into the essence of cognition, then whatever status it and our doubts about its reaching the object may have one thing is clear: that cognition itself is a name for a manifold sphere of being which can be given to us absolutely, and which can be given absolutely each time in the particular case. The thought processes which I really perform are given to me insofar as I *reflect* upon them, receive them and set them up in a *pure* "seeing." I can speak vaguely about cognition, perception, imagination, experience, judgment, inference, etc.; but then, when I reflect, all that is given, and absolutely given at that, is this phenomenon of vaguely "talking about and intending cognition, experience, judgment, etc." Even this phenomenon of vagueness is one of those that comes under the heading of cognition in the broadest sense. I can, however, have an actual perception and inspect it. I can, moreover, represent to myself in imagination or memory a perception and survey it as so given to imagination. In that case I am no longer / vacuously talking ‹31› about perception or having a vague intension or idea of it. Instead, perception itself stands open to my inspection as actually or imaginatively given to me. And the same is true of every intellectual process, of every form of thinking and cognizing.

I have here put on the same level the "seeing" [act of] reflective perception and [the "seeing" act of reflective] imagination. If one followed the Cartesian view, one would have to emphasize perception first; it would in some measure correspond to the so-called inner perception of traditional epistemology, though this is an ambivalent concept.

Every intellectual process and indeed every mental process whatever, while being enacted, *can be made the object of a pure "seeing" and understanding, and is something absolutely given in this "seeing."* It is given as something that is, that is here and now, and whose being cannot be sensibly doubted. To be sure, I can wonder what sort of being this is and how this mode of being is related to other modes. It is true I can wonder what givenness means *here*, and reflecting further I can "see" the "seeing" itself in which this givenness, or this mode of being, is constituted. But all the same I am now working on an absolute foundation: namely, this perception is, and remains as long as it lasts, something absolute, something here and now, something that in itself is what it is, something by which I can measure as by an ultimate standard what being and being given can mean and here must mean, at least, obviously, as far as the sort of being and being given is concerned which a "here and now" exemplifies. And that goes for all specific ways of thinking, whenever they are given. All of these, however, can also be data in imagination; they can "as it were" stand before our eyes and yet not stand before them as actualities, as actually accomplished perceptions, judgments, etc.; even then, they are, in a certain sense, data. They are there *open to intuition*. We talk about them not in just vague hints and empty intention. We inspect them, and while inspecting them we can observe their essence, their constitution, their intrinsic character, and we can make our speech conform in a pure measure to what is "seen" in its full clarity. But this requires to
‹32› be supplemented / by a discussion of the concept and cognition of essences.

For the moment we keep it firmly in mind that a sphere of

the absolutely given can be indicated at the outset; and this is just the sphere we need if it is to be possible to aim at a theory of knowledge. Indeed, lack of clarity with regard to the meaning or essence of cognition requires a science of cognition, a science whose sole end is to clarify the essential nature of cognition. It is not to explain cognition as a psychological fact; it is not to inquire into the natural causes and laws of the development and occurrence of cognitions. Such inquiry is the task of a science of the natural sort, of a psychology which deals with the mental processes of persons who are undergoing them. Rather, the task of the critique of cognition is to clarify, to cast light upon, the essence of cognition and the legitimacy of its claim to validity that belongs to its essence; and what else can this mean but to make the essence of cognition directly self-given.

Recapitulation and Amplification. In its constantly successful progress in the various sciences, cognition of the natural sort is altogether self-assured that it reaches the object and has no cause to worry about the possibility of cognition and about the meaning of cognized objectivity. But as soon as we begin to reflect on the correlation between cognition and reality (and eventually also on the ideal meanings on the one hand and, on the other, on the objects of cognition) there arise difficulties, absurdities, inconsistent yet seemingly well-founded theories which drive one to the admission that the possibility of cognition as far as its reaching the object is concerned is an enigma.

A new science, the critique of cognition, is called for. Its job is to resolve confusions and to clarify the essence of cognition. Upon the success of this science depends the possibility of a metaphysics, a science of being in the absolute and fundamental sense. But how / can such a science of cognition in general get <33> started? That which a science questions it cannot use as a presupposition. But what is in question is the possibility of all cognition in that the critique of cognition regards as problematic the possibility of cognition in general and its capacity to reach the object. Once it is launched, the critique of cognition cannot take any cognition for granted. Nor can it take over anything whatever from pre-scientific cognition. All cognition bears the mark of being questionable.

Without some cognition given at the outset, there is also no advancement of cognition. The critique of cognition cannot, therefore, begin. There can be no such science at all.

I already suggested that in all this there is an element of truth. In the beginning no cognition can be assumed *without examination*. However, even if the critique of cognition must not take over any antecedent cognition it still can begin by *giving* itself cognition, and naturally cognition which it does not base on, or logically derive from, anything else as this would presuppose some other immediate cognition already given. It must rather base itself on the cognition which is immediately evident and of such a kind that, as absolutely clear and indubitable, it excludes every doubt of its possibility and contains none of the puzzles which had led to all the sceptical confusions. I then pointed to the *Cartesian method of doubt* and to the domain of the absolutely given, viz., of absolute cognition which comes under the heading of evidence (*Evidenz*) of the *cogitatio*. It remained to be shown that the *immanence* of this cognition makes it an appropriate point of departure for the theory of cognition; that, furthermore, *because of this immanence*, it is free of the puzzlement which is the source of all sceptical embarrassment. Finally, it remained to be shown *that immanence is the generally necessary characteristic of all epistemological cognition*, and that it is nonsensical not only at the start but also in general to borrow from the sphere of transcendence, in other words, to try to found the theory of cognition on psychology or on any science whatever of the natural sort.

<34>   I may add the following: there is a plausible argument / to the effect that the theory of knowledge cannot get started because it questions cognition as such and hence regards as questionable every cognition with which we might begin. Moreover, it is alleged that if all cognition must be a riddle to the epistemologist, so must any initial cognition with which epistemology itself begins be a riddle. I repeat that this plausible argument is a deception. The deception is due to the vague generality of the wording. Cognition in general "is questioned." Surely, however, it is not denied that there is cognition in general (such denial would lead to contradiction); rather, cognition presents a certain problem, namely, of how it can accomplish a certain task attributed to it, namely, the task of reaching the object: I may even doubt whether this task can be accomplished at all. But doubt as I

may, this doubt is a first step toward canceling itself out because some cognitions can be brought to light which render such doubt groundless. Moreover, if I begin by not understanding cognition at all, then this incomprehension with its indeterminate universality admittedly encompasses every cognition. But that is not to say that every cognition I might run up against in the future has to remain forever incomprehensible. It may be that there is a big puzzle to begin with connected with a particular class of cognitions, those that thrust themselves most immediately to the fore, and that I now reach a general embarrassment and say: cognition as such is a riddle, even though it soon appears that the riddle does not belong to certain other kinds of cognition. And, as we shall see presently, this is indeed the case.

I said that the cognitions with which the critique of cognition must begin must contain nothing doubtful or questionable. They must contain none of that which precipitates epistemological confusion and gives impetus to the critique of cognition. We have to show that this holds true of the sphere of the *cognitio*. For this we need a more deeply probing reflection, one that will bring us substantial advantages.

If we look closer at what is so enigmatic and what, in the course of subsequent reflection on the possibility of cognition, causes embarrassment, we will find it to be the transcendence of cognition. All cognition of the natural sort, and especially the pre-scientific, is cognition which makes its object transcendent. / It ‹35› posits objects as existent, claims to reach matters of fact which are not "strictly given to it," are not "immanent" to it.

But on closer view, this *transcendence* is admittedly *ambiguous*. One thing one can mean by transcendence is that the object of cognition is not genuinely (*reell*) contained in the cognitive act so that one would be meaning by "being truly given" or "immanently given" that the object of the cognitive act is genuinely contained in the act: the cognitive act, the *cognitio*, has genuine abstract parts genuinely constituting it: but the physical thing which it intends or supposedly perceives or remembers, etc., is, not to be found in the *cognitio* itself, as a mental process; the physical thing is not to be found as a genuine (*reell*) concrete part (*Stück*), not as something which really exists within the *cognitio*. So the question is: how can the mental process so to speak transcend itself? *Immanent here means then genuinely (reell) immanent in the cognitive mental process.*

But there is still *another transcendence* whose opposite is an altogether different immanence, namely, *absolute* and *clear givenness, self-givenness in the absolute sense.* This givenness, which rules out any meaningful doubt, consists of a simply immediate "seeing" and apprehending of the intended object itself as it is, and it constitutes the precise concept of evidence (*Evidenz*) understood as immediate evidence. All cognition which is not evident, which though it intends or posits something objective yet *does not see it itself,* is transcendent in this second sense. In such cognition we go beyond what at any time *is truly given,* beyond what can be *directly "seen"* and *apprehended.* At this point we may ask: How can cognition posit something as existing that is not directly and truly given in it?

At first, before we come to a deeper level of critical epistemological reflection, these two kinds of immanence and transcendence run confusedly into each other. It is indeed clear that whoever raises the first question about the possibility of genuine (*reell*) transcendence is at the same time really also raising the second question: namely, how can there be transcendence beyond the realm of evident givenness? In this there is the unspoken supposition that the only actually understandable, unquestionable, absolutely evident givenness is the givenness of *the abstract part genuinely (reell) contained* within the cognitive ‹36› act, / and this is why anything in the way of a cognized objectivity that is not genuinely (*reell*) contained within that act is regarded as a puzzle and as problematic. We shall soon hear that this is a fatal mistake.

One may now construe transcendence in one sense or the other, or, at first even ambiguously, but transcendence is both the initial and the central problem of the critique of cognition. It is the riddle that stands in the path of cognition of the natural sort and is the incentive for new investigations. One could at the outset designate the solution to this problem as being the task of the critique of cognition. One would thereby delimit the new discipline in a preliminary fashion, instead of generally designating as its theme the problem of the essence of any cognition whatever.

If then the riddle connected with the initial establishment of the discipline lies *here*, it becomes more definitely clear what must not be claimed as presupposed. Nothing transcendent must be used as a presupposition. If I do not understand *how* it is possible that cognition reach something transcendent, then I also do not know *whether* it is possible. The scientific warrant for believing in a transcendent existence is of no help. For every mediated warrant goes back to something immediate; and it is the unmediated which contains the riddle.

Still someone might say: "It is certain that mediated no less than immediate cognition contains the riddle. But it is only the *how* that is puzzling, whereas the *that* is absolutely certain. No sensible man will doubt the existence of the world, and the sceptic in action belies his own creed." Very well. Then let us answer him with a more powerful and far-reaching argument. For it proves that the theory of cognition has, *neither at the outset nor throughout its course,* any license to fall back upon the content of the sciences of a natural sort which treat their object as transcendent. What is proved is the fundamental thesis *that the theory of knowledge can never be based upon any science of the natural sort, no matter what the more specific nature of that science may be.* Hence we ask: What will our opponent do with his transcendent knowledge? We put freely at his disposal the entire stock of transcendent truths contained in the objective / sciences, ‹37› and we take it that those truths are not altered by the emergence of the puzzle of how a science of the transcendent is possible. What will he now do with his all-embracing knowledge? How does he think he can go from the "that" to the "how"? That he knows for a fact that cognition of the transcendent is actual guarantees as logically obvious that cognition of the transcendent is possible. But the riddle is, *how* is it possible? Can he solve it even if he presupposes all the sciences, all or any cognition of the transcendent? Consider: What more does he really need? That cognition of the transcendent is possible he takes for granted, even as analytically certain in saying to himself, there is in my case knowledge of the transcendent. What he lacks is obvious. He is unclear about the relation to transcendence. He is unclear about the "reaching the transcendent" which is ascribed to cognition, to knowledge. Where and how can he achieve clarity?

He could do so if the essences of this relation were somehow *given* to him, so that he could "see" it and could directly inspect the unity of cognition and its object, a unity denoted by the locution "reaching the object." He would thereby not only know this unity to be possible, but he would have this possibility clearly before him. The possibility itself counts for him as something transcendent, as a possibility which is known but not of itself given, "seen." He obviously thinks: cognition is a thing apart from its object; cognition is given but the object of cognition is not given; and yet cognition is supposed to relate to the object, to cognize it. How can I understand this possibility? Naturally the reply is: I could understand it only if the relation itself were given as something to be "seen." As long as the object is, and remains, something transcendent, and cognition and its objects are actually separate, then indeed he can see nothing here, and his hopes for reaching a solution, perhaps even by way of falling back on transcendent presuppositions, are patent folly.

‹38›   However, if he is to be consistent with these views, he should give up his starting point: he should acknowledge that in this case cognition of the transcendent is impossible, and that his pretence to know is mere prejudice. Then the problem is no longer: How is cognition of the transcendent possible? But rather, How do we account for the prejudice which ascribes a transcendent feat to cognition? And this exactly was the path Hume took.

Let us emphatically reject that approach and let us go on to illustrate the basic idea that the problem of the "how" (how cognition of the transcendent is possible and even more generally, how cognition is possible at all) can never be answered on the basis of a prior knowledge of the transcendent, of prior judgments about it, no matter whence the knowledge or the judgments are borrowed, not even if they are taken from the exact sciences. Here is an illustration: A man born deaf knows that there are sounds, that sounds produce harmonies and that a splendid art depends upon them. But he cannot understand *how* sounds do this, how musical compositions are possible. Such things he cannot *imagine,* i.e., he cannot "see" and in "seeing" grasp the "how" of such things. His knowledge about what exists helps him in no way, and it would be absurd if he were to try to deduce the *how* of music from his knowledge, thinking that thereby he could achieve clarity about the possibility of music through conclusions drawn from things of which he is cognizant. It will not do to draw conclusions from existences of which one knows but which one cannot "see." "Seeing" does not lend itself to demonstration or deduction. It is patently absurd to try to explain possibilities (and unmediated possibilities at that) by drawing logical conclusions from non-intuitive knowledge. Even if I could be wholly certain that there are transcendent worlds, even if I accept the whole content of the sciences of a natural sort, even then I cannot borrow from them. I must never fancy that by relying on transcendent presuppositions and scientific inferences I can arrive where I want to go in the critique of cognition — namely, to assess the possibility of a transcendent objectivity of cognition. And that goes not just for the beginning but for the whole course of the critique of cognition, so long as there still remains the problem of *how cognition is possible*. | And, ‹39› evidently, that goes not just for the problem of transcendent objectivity but also for the elucidation of every possibility.

If we combine this with the extraordinarily strong inclination to make a transcendently oriented judgment and thus to fall into a μετάβασις εἰς ἄλλο γένος [a change into some other kind] in every case where a thought process involves transcendence and a judgment has to be based upon it, then we arrive at a sufficient and complete deduction of the *epistemological principle* that an epistemological *reduction* has to be accomplished in the case of every epistemological inquiry of whatever sort of cognition. That is to say, everything transcendent that is involved must be bracketed, or be assigned the index of indifference, of epistemological nullity, an index which indicates: the existence of all these transcendencies, whether I believe in them or not, is not here my concern; this is not the place to make judgments about them; they are entirely irrelevant.

All the basic errors of the theory of knowledge go hand in hand with the above mentioned μετάβασις, on the one hand the basic error of psychologism, on the other that of anthropologism and biologism.[1] The μετάβασις is so exceedingly dangerous, partly

---

[1] Tr. note: Husserl's words are *Anthropologismus* and *Biologismus*, clearly coined to parallel *Psychologismus* (Psychologism).

because the proper sense of the problem is never made clear and remains totally lost in it, and partly because even those who have become clear about it find it hard to remain clear and slip easily, as their thinking proceeds, back into the temptations of the natural modes of thought and judgment as well as into the false and seductive conceptions of the problems which grow on their basis.

LECTURE III <41>

By these considerations what the critique of cognition may and <43>
may not use has been precisely and adequately determined. What
is especially puzzling for such a critique is the possibility of
transcendence, but it may never under any conditions exploit
for its purposes the actuality of transcendent things. Obviously
the sphere of usable objects or of cognitions is limited to those
which present themselves as valid, and which can remain free of
the marks of epistemological vacuity; but this sphere is not
empty. We have indubitably secured the whole realm of *cogitationes*. The existence of the *cogitatio*, more precisely the phenomenon of cognition itself, is beyond question; and it is free from
the riddle of transcendence. These existing things are already
presupposed in the statement of the problem of cognition. The
question as to how transcendent things come into cognition
would lose its sense if cognition itself, as well as the transcendent
object, were put in question. It is also clear that the *cogitationes*
present a sphere of *absolutely immanent data; it is in this sense that
we understand "immanence."* In the "seeing" pure phenomena the
object is not outside cognition or outside "consciousness," while
being given in the sense of the absolute self-givenness of something which is simply "seen."

But here we need assurance through *epistemological reduction*,
the methodological essence of which we now want to examine *in
concreto* for the first time. We need the reduction at this point in
order to prevent the evidence of the existence of the *cogitatio*
from being confused with the evidence that *my cogitatio* exists,
with the evidence of the *sum cogitans*, and the like. One must
guard himself from the fundamental confusion between the *pure
phenomenon*, in the sense of phenomenology, and the *psychological phenomenon*, the object of empirical psychology. If I, as a

human being employing my natural modes of thought, look at
<44> the perception which I am undergoing at the moment, / then I
immediately and almost inevitably apperceive it (that is a fact)
in relation to my ego. It stands there as a mental process of this
mentally living person, as his state, his act; the sensory content
stands there as what is given or sensed, as that of which I am
conscious; and it integrates itself with the perception of objective
time. Perception, and any other *cogitatio*, so apperceived, is a
psychological fact. Thus it is apperceived as a datum in objective
time, belonging to the mentally living ego, the ego which is in
the world and lasts through its duration (a duration which is
measured by means of empirically calibrated timepieces). This,
then, is the phenomenon which is investigated by that natural
science we call "psychology."

The phenomenon in this sense falls under the principle to
which we must subject ourselves in the critique of cognition, the
principle of the ἐποχή, which holds for everything transcendent.
The ego as a person, as a thing in the world, and the mental life
as the mental life of this person, are arranged — no matter even
if quite indefinitely — on objective time; they are all transcendent and epistemologically null. Only through a reduction, the
same one we have already called *phenomenological reduction*, do I
attain an absolute datum which no longer presents anything
transcendent. Even if I should put in question the ego and the
world and the ego's mental life as such, still my simply "seeing"
reflection on what is given in the apperception of the relevant
mental process and on my ego, yields the *phenomenon* of this
apperception; the phenomenon, so to say, of "perception construed as my perception." Of course, I can also make use of the
natural mode of reflection here, and relate this phenomenon to
my ego, postulating this ego as an empirical reality through
saying again: I have this phenomenon, it is mine. Then, in order
to get back to the pure phenomenon, I would have to put the
ego, as well as time and the world once more into question, and
thereby display a pure phenomenon, the pure *cogitatio*. But while
I am perceiving I can also look, by way of purely "seeing," at
the perception, at it itself as it is there, and ignore its relation
to the ego, or at least abstract from it. Then the perception which
is thereby grasped and delimited in "seeing," is an absolutely

given, pure phenomenon in the phenomenological sense, re-
nouncing anything transcendent.

Thus to each psychic lived process there corresponds through the ‹45›
device of phenomenological reduction a pure phenomenon, which
exhibits its intrinsic (immanent) essence (raken individually) *as an*
absolute datum. Every postulation of a "non-immanent actuality," of anything which is not contained in the phenomenon, even
if intended by the phenomenon, and which is therefore not given
in the second sense, is bracketed, i.e., suspended.

If it is possible to take such phenomena for objects of investigation, then it is obvious that we are now no longer within
psychology, within a natural, transcendently "objectivizing"
science. Then we do not investigate and speak of psychological
phenomena, of certain happenings in so-called real actuality (the
existence of which remains throughout in question), but of that
which exists and is valid whether there is such a thing as objective actuality or not, whether the postulation of such transcendent entities is justifiable or not. Thus at this point we speak
of such absolute data; even if these data are related to objective
actuality via their intentions, their intrinsic character is *within*
them; nothing is assumed concerning *the existence or non-ex-*
istence of actuality. And so we have dropped anchor on the shore
of phenomenology, the existence of the objects of which is assured, as the objects of a scientific investigation should be; not,
however, in the manner of components of the ego or of the
temporal world, but rather as absolute data grasped in purely
immanent "seeing." And this pure immanence is first of all to be
characterized, in our approach, through *phenomenological*
reduction: I mean, not with respect to what it refers to beyond
itself, but with respect to what it is in itself and to what it is
given as. All this discussion is, of course, only a roundabout way
of helping one to see what is to be seen in this regard, viz., the
distinction between the quasi-givenness of transcendent objects
and the absolute givenness of the phenomenon itself.

But we must take new steps, enter onto new considerations, so
that we may gain a firm foothold in the new land and not finally
run aground on its shore. For this shore / has its rocks, and over ‹46›
it lie clouds of obscurity which threaten us with stormy gales of
scepticism. What we have said up to this point holds for all

phenomena, although for purposes of the critique of reason, we are, naturally, interested only in cognitive phenomena. Thus the results set forth below can just as well be applied to all phenomena, as they hold *mutatis mutandis* for all of them.

In our quest for a critique of cognition, we have been led to a beginning, to a stronghold of data which is at our disposal, and it appears that this is what we need above all. If I am to fathom the essence of cognition, then I must, of course, possess cognition in all its questionable forms, *as a datum*, and possess it in such a way that this datum has in itself nothing of the problematic character which other cognitions bring with them, however much they seem to offer us data.

Having assured ourselves of the field of pure cognition, we can now investigate it and start a science of pure phenomena, a *phenomenology*. Is it not obvious that this must be the basis for the solution to the problems which have been agitating us? Thus it is clear that I can only attain insight into the essence of cognition if I look at it myself, and if it itself is given to me to "see," as it really is. I must study it immanently and by pure inspection within the pure phenomenon, within "pure consciousness." To be sure, its transcendence is doubtful; the existence of objects to which it is related insofar as it is transcendent, is not given to me; and questions are raised precisely as to how, in spite of this, they can be postulated, and as to what significance it has and must have if such postulation is to be possible. On the other hand, even if I raise questions about the existence and reaching the object of this relation to transcendent things, still it has something which can be grasped in the pure phenomenon. The relating-itself-to-transcendent-things, whether it is meant in this or that way, is still an inner feature of the phenomenon. It almost seems as if it would depend only on a science of absolute *cogitationes*. Since I have to cancel out any previous acceptance of the intended transcendent objects, where else could I investigate both the *meaning* of this intending-something-beyond, and also, along with this meaning, its possible *validity*, or the meaning of such validity? Where else but the place at which this meaning is un-
‹47› qualifiedly given / and at which in the pure phenomenon of relation, corroboration, justification the meaning of validity, for its part, comes to absolute givenness.

To be sure, we are overtaken here once more by the doubt whether there is not still a surplus which must pass over into action, whether the datum of validity does not carry with it the givenness of the object, which, on the other hand, could not be the givenness of the *cogitatio*, at least insofar as there is really such a thing as valid transcendence. Nevertheless a science of absolute phenomena, understood as *cogitationes*, is the first thing we need, and this has to produce at least a major part of the solution.

Thus, it must be our aim to set up a phenomenology, more specifically a phenomenology of cognitions, construed as a theory of the essence of pure cognitive phenomena. The outlook is favorable. But how is phenomenology to proceed? How is it possible? I am supposed to make assertions, indeed objectively valid assertions; I am supposed to cognize pure phenomena scientifically. *But does all science not lead to the establishing of objects existing in themselves, i.e., to transcendent objects?* What is scientifically established is something which is what it is in itself; it is to be accepted just as existing whether I, in my cognition, postulate it as existing or not. Does not science by its very essence have as its correlate the objectivity of that which is known only in science, and which is scientifically established? And that which is scientifically established is universally valid, is it not? But what is the situation here? We move in the field of pure phenomena. But why do I say *field?* It is more nearly a *Heraclitean flux* of phenomena. What assertions can I make about it? Now, while "seeing," I can say: this here: No doubt it is. Perhaps I can further say that this phenomenon includes that one as a part, or is connected to that one; this one spreads over that one, etc.

But obviously there is no *"objective validity"* to these assertions; they have *no "objective meaning"*; they have a merely *"subjective" truth.* Now we do not wish to become involved here in an attempt to determine whether there is not a sense in which these assertions have a certain objectivity, even while they can be pronounced "subjectively" true. But it is already clear to a fleeting glance that that higher dignity of objectivity, which the prescientific natural / judgment dramatizes, so to speak, and ‹48› which the considered judgments of the exact sciences bring to an incomparably higher fulfillment, is altogether lacking here. We shall not attribute any special value to such assertions — that this is here, etc. — which we make on the basis of pure "seeing."

Moreover we are reminded here of the famous Kantian distinction between *judgments of perceptions* and *judgments of experience*. The relationship is obvious. However, as Kant lacked the concepts of phenomenology and phenomenological reduction, and as he had not been able to completely escape psychologism and anthropologism, he did not arrive at the ultimate significance of the distinction which is necessary here. Naturally with us it is not a question of merely subjectively valid judgments which are limited in their validity to the empirical subject, or even of objective validity in the sense of validity for every subject without restriction. Indeed we have bracketed the empirical subject; and the transcendental apperception, consciousness as such, will soon acquire for us a completely different meaning, one which is not at all mysterious.

Let us now return to the main theme of our discussion. Phenomenological judgments, if restricted to singular judgments, do not have very much to teach us. But how are judgments, particularly scientifically valid judgments, to be established? And the word *scientific* immediately puts us into an embarrassing position. Does objectivity not carry *transcendence* with it, and along with this also the doubt as to what it is supposed to signify, as to *whether* and how it is possible? Through *epistemological reduction* we exclude transcendent presuppositions, because transcendence is in question with respect to its possible validity and its meaning. But then are the scientific or transcendent conclusions of the theory of knowledge themselves still possible? Is it not obvious that before the possibility of transcendence is established no transcendent result of the theory of knowledge can itself be secure? But if, as it might seem, the epistemological ἐποχή demands that we accept nothing transcendent until we have established its possibility, and if the establishing of the possibility of transcendence itself, as an objective result, requires

‹49› transcendent postulations, then it seems / that we are faced with the prospect of a circle, which makes phenomenology and the theory of knowledge impossible; and the labor of love in which we have been engaged up to this point will have been in vain.

We cannot, without more ado, despair of the possibility of a phenomenology and of what is obviously bound up with that in this discussion — a critique of cognition. What we need at this point is a further step which will unroll this spurious circle for us. We have already accomplished this in principle, for we distinguished two senses of transcendence and of immanence. After Descartes had established the evidence of the *cogitatio* (or rather of the *cogito ergo sum*, a conception which we have not adopted), he asked, as you will recall: *What is it which assures me of these fundamental data?* The answer is: the *clara et distincta perceptio.*[1] We can carry this further. I need not claim that we already have a purer and deeper grasp of the matter than Descartes, and that thereby we grasp and understand [the concept of] evidence, the *clara et distincta perceptio*, in a more exact sense. With Descartes we can now take the further step (*mutatis mutandis*): to whatever is given through a *clara et distincta perceptio*, as each *cogitatio* is, we may accord an equal validity. To be sure, if we recall the third and fourth Meditations, the proofs of the existence of God, the appeal to the *veracitas dei*,[2] etc., we can expect difficulties. Therefore, be very sceptical, or rather critical.

We have the givenness of the pure *cogitatio* as an absolute possession, but not the givenness of outer things in external perception, although such perception makes a claim to be giving the existence of these things. The transcendence of things requires that we put them in question. We do not understand how perception can reach transcendent objects, but we understand how perception can reach the immanent, provided it is reflective and purely immanent perception which has undergone reduction. But what enables us to understand this? Well, we directly "see," we directly grasp what we intend in the act of "seeing" and grasping. To have a phenomenon before one's eyes, which points to something which is not itself given in the phenomenon, and then to doubt whether such an object exists, and if so how it is to be understood that it exists — this is meaningful. But to "see" and to intend absolutely nothing more than what is grasped in "seeing," and then still / to question and doubt, that is nonsense. <50> Basically what I am saying amounts to this. The "seeing" or

1 Tr. note: Clear and distinct perception.
2 Tr. note: The veracity of God.

grasping of what is given, insofar as it is actual "seeing," actual self-givenness in the strictest sense and not another sort of givenness which points to something which is not given — that is an ultimate. That is *absolute self-evidence;* if you are looking for what is not self-evident, what is problematic, or perhaps entirely mysterious, consider the reference to something transcendent, i.e., intention, belief, even a detailed proof of something not given. And it does not help us that even here an absolute datum can be found — the givenness of intention and belief themselves. To be sure, if we only reflect we will find this before us; but what is given here is not what was intended.

But can it be that absolute self-evidence, self-givenness in "seeing," is realized only in particular mental processes and their particular abstract aspects and parts, i.e., only in the "seeing" grasp of the *here and now?* Would there not have to be a "seeing" grasp of other data as absolute data, e.g., universals, in such a way that were a universal to attain self-evident givenness within "seeing," any doubt about it would then be absurd?

How remarkable it would be to limit the *cogitatio* to pheno-menologically singular data can be seen from this fact, that the whole doctrine of evidence, which we, following Descartes, have set forth, and which certainly is illuminated with absolute clarity and self-evidence, would lose its value. That is, concerning the case of a *cogitatio* which lies before us as something particular, perhaps a feeling which we are now undergoing, one might say: this is given. But we would by no means dare to put forward the most universal proposition: *the givenness of any reduced phenomenon is an absolute and indubitable givenness.*

But this is only to help you along. In any event, it is illuminating that the possibility of a critique of cognition depends on the demonstration of absolute data which are different from even the reduced *cogitationes.* To view the matter more precisely, in the subject-predicate judgments which we make concerning them, we have already gone beyond them. If we say: this phenomenon of judgment underlies this or that phenomenon of <51> imagination, this / perceptual phenomenon contains this or that aspect, color content, etc., and even if, just for the sake of argument, we make these assertions in the most exact conformity with the givenness of the *cogitatio,* then the logical forms which we employ, and which are reflected in the linguistic expressions themselves, already go beyond the mere *cogitationes*. A "something more" is involved which does not at all consist of a mere agglomeration of new *cogitationes*. And even if predicational thinking gives rise to new *cogitationes*, which are joined to those concerning which we made the assertions, nevertheless they are not what constitute the predicational facts which are the objective correlates of the assertions.

That cognition, which can bring to *absolute self-givenness* not only particulars, but also *universals, universal objects, and universal states of affairs*, is more easily conceivable, at least for anyone who can assume the position of pure "seeing" and can hold all natural prejudices at arm's length. This cognition is of decisive significance for the possibility of phenomenology. For its special character consists in the fact that it is the analysis of essence and the investigation into essence in the area of pure "seeing" thought and absolute self-givenness. That is necessarily its character; it sets out to be a science and a method which will explain possibilities — possibilities of cognition and possibilities of valuation — and will explain them in terms of their fundamental essence. They are generally questionable possibilities, and investigations of them must take on the character of general investigations of essence. Analysis of essence is *eo ipso* general analysis; cognition of essence in terms of essence, in terms of essential nature, in terms of cognition which is directed to universal objects. It is here that talk of the *a priori* has its legitimate place. For what does *a priori* cognition mean except a cognition which is directed to general essences, and which entirely bases its absolute validity on essence, at least insofar as we exclude the discredited empiricist concept of the *a priori*.

In any event, although this may be the only justifiable concept of the *a priori*, another one can be found if we range under the heading of the *a priori* all concepts which as categories have a principal meaning in a certain sense, and then in addition the essential principles which are based on these concepts.

If we concentrate here on the first concept of the *a priori*, then <52> phenomenology will have to do with the *a priori* in the sphere of origins and of absolute data, with species grasped in general 'seeing," and with the *a priori* truths which these species render immediately "seeable." When we engage in the critique of reason, not only the theoretical, but also the practical and any other kind, the chief goal is certainly the *a priori* in the second sense; it is to establish the principal self-given forms and facts and, by means of this self-givenness, to develop, interpret, and evaluate the concepts which come forward with a claim to crucial significance, as well as the principles of logic, ethics, and theory of value.

If we restrict ourselves to the pure phenomenology of cog- <55> nition, then we will be concerned with the *essence of cognition as* revealed in direct "seeing," i.e., with a demonstration of it which is carried out by way of "seeing" in the sphere of phenomenological reduction and self-givenness, and with an analytical distinction between the various sorts of phenomena which are embraced by the very broad term "cognition." Then the question is as to what is essentially contained and grounded in them, from what factors they are built up, what possibilities of combination can be found while remaining purely within their essential natures, and what general interrelations flow from their essences.

And it is not merely concerned with the genuinely (*reell*) immanent, but also with what is *immanent in the itentional sense*. Cognitive mental processes (and this belongs to their essence) have an *intentio*, they refer to something, they are related in this or that way to an object. This activity of relating itself to an object belongs to them even if the object itself does not. And what is objective can appear, can have a certain kind of givenness in appearance, even though it is at the same time neither genuinely (*reell*) within the cognitive phenomenon, nor does it exist in any other way as a *cogitatio*. To explain the essence of cognition and the essential connections which belong to it and to bring this to self-givenness, this involves examining both these sides of the matter; it involves investigating this relatedness which belongs to the essence of cognition. And just here lie the puzzles, the mysteries, the problems concerning the ultimate meaning of the objectivity of cognition, including its reaching or failing to reach the object, if it is judgmental cognition and its adequacy, if it is evident cognition, etc.

In any case, the whole investigation into essence, is in fact, obviously a general investigation. The particular cognitive phenomenon, coming and going in the stream of consciousness, is not the sort of thing about which phenomenology establishes its ⟨56⟩ conclusions. Phenomenology is directed to the / "sources of cognition," to general origins which can be "seen," to general absolute data which present the universal basic criteria in terms of which all meaning, and also the correctness, of confused thinking is to be evaluated, and by which all the riddles which have to do with the objectivity of cognition are to be solved.

Still, are real *universality*, universal essences, and the universal states of affairs attaching to them capable of self-givenness in the same sense as a *cogitatio? Does not the universal as such transcend knowledge?* Knowledge of universals is certainly given as an absolute phenomenon; but in this we shall seek in vain for the universal which is to be identical, in the strictest sense, in the equally immanent contents of innumerable possible cases of cognition.

Of course, we answer, as we have already answered: to be sure, the universal has this kind of transcendence. Every genuine (*reell*) constituent of the cognitive phenomenon, this phenomenological particular, is also a particular; and so the universal, which certainly is no particular, cannot be really contained in the consciousness of the universal. But the objection to *this* kind of transcendence is nothing more than a prejudice, which stems from an inappropriate interpretation of cognition, one which is not based on the source of cognition. Thus one has to get especially clear about the fact that we accord the status of absolute self-givenness to the absolute phenomenon, the *cogitatio* which has undergone reduction. not because it is a particular, but because it displays itself in pure "seeing" after phenomenological reduction, *precisely as absolute self-givenness*. But in pure "seeing" we find that universality no less displays *just* such an absolute givenness.

Is this actually the case? Let us now consider some cases in which a universal is given, i.e., cases where a purely immanent consciousness of the universal is built up on the basis of some "seen" and self-given particular. I have a particular intuition of redness, or rather several such intuitions. I stick strictly to the pure immanence; I am careful to perform the phenomenological

reduction. I snip off any further significance of redness, any way
in which it may be viewed as something transcendent, e.g., as
the redness of a piece of blotting paper / on my table, etc. And <57>
now I fully grasp in pure "seeing" the *meaning* of the concept of
redness in general, redness *in specie*, the *universal* "seen" as
identical in this and that. No longer is it the particular as such
which is referred to, not this or that red thing, but redness in
general. If we really did this in pure "seeing," could we then still
intelligibly doubt what redness is in general, what is meant by
this expression, what it may be in its very essence? We truly
"see" it; there it is, the very object of our intent, this species of
redness. Could a deity, an infinite intellect, do more to lay hold of
the essence of redness than to "see" it as a universal?

And if now perhaps two species of redness are given to us, two
shades of red, can we not judge that this and that are similar to
each other, not this particular, individual phenomenon of redness,
but the type, the shade as such? Is not the relation of similarity
here a general absolute datum?

Again, this givenness is also something purely immanent, not
immanent in the spurious sense, i.e., existing in the sphere of an
individual consciousness. We are not speaking at all of the act of
abstraction in the psychological subject, and of the psychological
conditions under which this takes place. We are speaking of the
general essence of meaning of redness and its givenness in general
"seeing."

Thus it is now senseless still to raise questions and doubts as to
what the essence of redness is, or what the meaning of redness is,
provided that while one "sees" redness and grasps it in its specific
character, one means by the word "red" just exactly that which
is being grasped and "seen" there. And in the same way it is
senseless, with respect to the essence of cognition and the fundamental structure of cognition, to wonder what its meaning is,
provided one is immediately given the paradigmatic phenomena
and the type in question in a purely "seeing" and eidetic (*ideieren-
der*) reflection within the sphere of phenomenological reduction.
However, cognition is certainly not so simple a thing as redness; a
great many forms and types of it are to be distinguished. And not
only that; their essential relations to one another need to be
investigated. For to understand cognition we must generally

<58> clarify the *teleological interconnections* within cognition, / which amount to certain essential relations of different essential types of intellectual forms. And here belongs also the ultimate explanation of the principles which, as ideal conditions of the possibility of scientific objectivity, function as norms governing the whole enterprise of empirical science. This whole attempt at the explanation of principles moves throughout in the sphere of essence, which is repeatedly built up (*konstituiert*) on the basis of particular phenomena through phenomenological reduction.

At every point this analysis is an analysis of essences and an investigation of the general states of affairs which are to be built up in immediate intuition. Thus the whole investigation is an *a priori* one, though, of course, it is not *a priori* in the sense of mathematical deductions. What distinguishes it from the "objectivizing" *a priori* sciences is its methods and its goal. *Phenomenology proceeds by "seeing," clarifying, and determining meaning, and by distinguishing meanings.* It compares, it distinguishes, it forms connections, it puts into relation, divides into parts, or distinguishes abstract aspects. But all within pure "seeing." It does not theorize or carry out mathematical operations; that is to say, it carries through no explanations in the sense of deductive theory. As it explains the basic concepts and propositions which function as principles governing the possibility of "objectivizing" science (but finally it also takes its own basic concepts and principles as objects of reflective explanation), it ends where "objectivizing" science begins. Hence it is a science in a completely different sense, and with completely different problems and methods. *The procedure of "seeing" and eidetic abstraction within the strictest phenomenological reduction is exclusively its own: it is the specifically philosophical method, insofar as this method belongs essentially to the meaning of the critique of cognition and so generally to every sort of critique of reason* (hence also evaluative and practical reason). But whatever is called philosophy in addition to the critique of reason in the strict <59> sense, is intimately related to this: metaphysics of / nature and metaphysics of all forms of mental life, and thus metaphysics in general in the widest sense.

In such cases one speaks of seeing something *evident*, and in fact those who recognize the pregnant concept of evidence and

take a firm grip on the essence of such evidence have these kinds
of occurrences exclusively in mind. The basic point is that one
must not overlook the fact that evidence is this consciousness
which is truly [a] "seeing" [consciousness] and which has a direct
and adequate grasp of itself and that signifies nothing other than
adequate self-givenness. The empiricist epistemologists, who
speak so much about the virtues of investigating origins, and with
all this remain as far from true origins as the most extreme
rationalist, would have us believe that the whole distinction between judgments that are evident and those that are not consists
of a certain feeling through which the former are marked out. But
what can a feeling do to give us an understanding of this matter?
What is it supposed to accomplish? Is it, so to speak, supposed to
call out to us: "Stop! Here is the truth?" But why then do we
have to trust this call? Must this trust also carry its credentials in
feeling? And why does a judgment with the meaning 2 times 2
equals 5 never have this mark in feeling? and why is it impossible
for it to have such a mark? Exactly how does one come to the
theory that the mark of truth resides in feeling? Well, one says
to oneself: "The same judgment, in the logical sense, e.g., the
judgment that 2 times 2 equals 4, can at one time be evident to
me and at another time not; the same concept of 4 can at one
time be given to me in luminous intuition (*intuitiv in Evidenz*)
and at another time in a merely symbolic representation. Thus
with respect to content, on both occasions we have the same
phenomenon, but on the one occasion there is a feeling which
marks it out and thereby lends it a superior status, a character of
validity." Have I in fact the same object on both occasions, except that on one occasion a feeling is given along with it, on the
other not? But if one directs his attention to the phenomenon,
he will notice at once that in actuality it is not the same phenomenon which lies before him on these two occasions, but two
essentially different phenomena, which have only one feature in
common. If I see that 2 times 2 equals 4, and then assert it in a
vague symbolic assertion, in the latter case I am referring to an
equality; but to refer to equality, that is not to have that phenomenon. The content of the two is different. One time I "see," and
in "seeing" the interrelation itself is given; the other time I
perform a symbolic reference. One time I have intuition; the
other time I have an empty intention.

<60>   Thus does the distinction amount to this, that in both cases something common is present, the same "meaning," once with a feeling-label and once without? Let one attend to the phenomenon itself, instead of going beyond to talk about it and interpret it. Let us take a simpler example: if I at a certain time have redness in a living intuition and at another time think about redness in terms merely of symbols with empty intention, is it then the case that both times the same phenomenon of redness is really present, only once with a feeling and once without?

Thus one needs only to look at the phenomena in order to recognize that they are completely different, united only through what identifies them as two cases of the same thing, which we call "meaning." But if the difference is to be found in the phenomena themselves, then what need have we of feeling as a principle of distinction? And does the distinction not lie precisely in this, that in one case the self-givenness of redness lies before us, the self-givenness of number and of the general equality of number — or, subjectively expressed, the adequate "seeing" grasp and possession of the entities themselves — while in the other case we have a mere reference to these things? And so we have no sympathy with this notion of feeling as evidence. It could be justified only if it were to display itself in pure "seeing," and if pure "seeing" were to signify just that which *we* attribute to it and which contradicts it.

Thus with respect to the application of the concept of evidence, we can now say: in the existence of the *cogitatio* we find evidence, and for that reason the *cogitatio* engenders no puzzles, not even the puzzle of transcendence. We accord it the status of something unquestionable, on the basis of which we may proceed further. No less do we find evidence in the universal; we recognize that *universal objects* and *states of affairs* attain self-givenness. And they are unquestionably given in the same sense; hence they are adequately self-given in the strictest sense of the term.

Hence phenomenological reduction does not entail a limitation of the investigation to the sphere of genuine (*reell*) immanence, to the sphere of that which is genuinely contained within the absolute this of the *cogitatio*. It entails no limitation to the sphere of the *cogitatio*. Rather it entails a limitation to the sphere of things that are *purely self-given*, to the sphere of those things

which are not merely spoken about, / meant, or perceived, but ‹61:
instead to the sphere of those things that are given in just
exactly the sense in which they are thought of, and moreover are
self-given in the strictest sense — in such a way that nothing
which is meant fails to be given. In a word, we are restricted to
the sphere of pure evidence, but understanding this term in a
certain strict sense, which definitely excludes any "mediate
evidence," and especially excludes all evidence in a loose sense.

Absolute givenness is an ultimate. Of course one can easily
say and insist that something is absolutely given to him when it
is not really the case. Again, absolute givenness can either be
vaguely spoken of, or can itself be given in absolute givenness.
Just as I can "see" a phenomenon of redness, and also can
merely talk about it without "seeing," so I can also either talk
about the "seeing" of redness or direct my "seeing" to the
"seeing" of redness, and so grasp the "seeing" of redness itself in
"seeing." On the other hand, to deny self-givenness in general
is to deny every ultimate norm, every basic criterion which gives
significance to cognition. But in that case one would have to
construe everything as illusion, and, in a nonsensical way, also
take illusion as such to be an illusion; and so one would altogether relapse into the absurdities of scepticism. However, it is
obvious that the only one who can argue in this way against the
sceptic is the man who *"sees"* the ultimate basis of knowledge,
who is willing to assign a significance to "seeing," inspecting
evidence. Whoever does not see or will not see, who talks and
argues, but always remains at the place where he accepts all
conflicting points of view and at the same time denies them all,
there is nothing we can do with him. We cannot answer: "obviously" it is the case. For he denies that there is any such thing
as "obviously." It is as if a blind man wished to deny that there
is such a thing as seeing, or still better, as if one who has sight
wished to deny that he himself sees and that there is any such
thing as seeing. How could we convince him, assuming that he
has no other mode of perception?

Thus if we hold fast to the absolute self-givenness of which we
already know that it does not signify the self-givenness of
genuine (*reell*) particulars, not even the absolute particulars of
the *cogitatio*, then the question arises as to how far it extends and

as to the extent to which, and the sense in which, it ties itself
<62> down to the sphere of *cogitationes* / and the universals which are
abstracted from them. If one has cast off the first and most
immediate prejudice, which sees the only absolute datum in the
particular *cogitatio* and in the sphere of genuinely (*reell*) immanent
things, one must now also do away with the further and no less
immediate prejudice, according to which newly self-given objects
spring up *only* in general intuitions derived from the sphere of
cogitationes.

"In reflective perception, the *cogitationes* are absolutely given
to us in that we consciously undergo them," so one would like to
begin. And then we can inspect universals which are singled out
within them and within their genuinely (*reell*) abstract aspects;
we can, in a "seeing" abstraction, grasp universals and the
essential connections which are solely grounded in them as self-
given states of affairs, constituted in "seeing"-interrelating
thought. That is the end of the matter.

Meanwhile no inclination is more dangerous to the "seeing"
cognition of origins and absolute data than to think too much,
and from these reflections in thought to create supposed self-
evident principles. Principles which for the most part are not at
all explicitly formulated and hence are not subject to any critique
based on "seeing" but rather implicitly determine and unjusti-
fiably limit the direction of investigation. *"Seeing" cognition is
that form of reason which sets itself the task of converting the understanding into reason.* The understanding is not to be allowed to
interrupt and to insert its unredeemed bank notes among the
certified ones; and its method of convertion and exchange, based
on mere treasury bonds, is not questioned here.

Thus as little interpretation as possible, but as pure an intuition as possible (*intuitio sine comprehensione*). In fact, we will
hark back to the speech of the mystics when they describe the
intellectual seeing which is supposed not to be a discursive
knowledge. And the whole trick consists in this — to give free
rein to the seeing eye and to bracket the references which go
beyond the "seeing" and are entangled with the seeing, along
with the entities which are supposedly given and thought along
with the "seeing," and, finally, to bracket what is read into them
through the accompanying reflections. The crucial question is:

Is the supposed object given in / the proper sense? Is it, in the <63>
strictest sense, "seen" and grasped, or does the intention go
beyond that?

Supposing this to be the case, we soon recognize that it would
be a *fiction* to believe that investigation by way of "seeing"
moves in the sphere of a so-called *inner perception* and in the
sphere of the purely immanent abstractions based on the phenomena and phenomenal aspects of inner perception. There are
many sorts of objectivity and, correlatively, many sorts of so-
called givenness. Perhaps the givenness of existents in the sense
of the so-called "inner perception," and again the givenness of the
existents in the natural, "objectivizing" sciences, is only one sort
of givenness; while the others, although labeled as nonexistent,
are still types of givenness. And it is only because they are, that
they can be set over against the other sorts and distinguished
from them in evidence.

<65>

LECTURE V

<67>   If we have firmly established the evidence of the *cogitatio*, and
then have conceded the further step of recognizing the evident
givenness of the universal, this step will at once lead us further.

By perceiving color and exercising reduction on this perception
I arrive at the pure phenomenon of color. And if I now achieve a
pure abstraction, I will get to the essence of phenomenological
color as such. But am I not equally in full possession of this
essence if I have a clear image?

As far as *memory* is concerned it is not anything simple, and
from the start it presents different forms of objects and, inter-
connected with these, different forms of givenness. Thus one
could refer to the so-called *primary memory*, the *retention* which is
necessarily bound up with every perception. The mental process
which we are now undergoing becomes objective to us in immediate reflection, and thenceforth it displays in reflection the
same objectivity: the self-same tone which has just existed as an
actual "now" remains henceforth the same tone, but moving
back into the past and there continually constituting the same
objective point in time. And if the tone does not cease but continues, and during its continuation presents itself as the same in
content or else as changing content, can we not grasp this fact —
that it remains the same or changes — evidently (within certain
limits)? And again, does this not mean that "seeing" *extends*
beyond the strictly present moment and hence is capable of
grasping intentionally, in continually new moments, what is no
longer existing, and that it is capable of becoming certain of a
stretch of past time in the manner of evident givenness? And
again we must distinguish, on the one hand, the pertinent object
which is and was, which endures and changes and, on the other
hand, the pertinent phenomenon of presentness and pastness,

of duration and change, which is from time to time a "now." It is
in the latter, and in the gradations it contains and the continual / <68>
changes it undergoes, that *temporal existence* is brought into
appearance and presented. The object is not a genuinely concrete
part of the phenomenon; in its temporality it has something
which cannot at all be found in the phenomenon or reduced to
the phenomenon. And yet it is constituted within the phenomenon. It is presented therein and is evidently given as "existing" there.

Further, as to the givenness of essences, it is constituted not
only on the basis of perception and the retention which is bound
up with it, in such a way that we, so to speak, pluck a universal
from the phenomenon itself; it is also constituted by *universalizing*
the object of appearance, positing a universal while gazing on it,
e.g., temporal content in general, duration in general, change in
general. Moreover, imagination and memory can also serve as its
foundation; they themselves present pure possibilities to be
grasped. In a similar way we can take from these acts universals
which, for their part, are not genuinely contained in these acts.

It is obvious that a fully evident grasp of essence *refers back* to
some particular intuition on the basis of which it must be built
up, but therefore *not necessarily to a particular perception*, which
has given us the paradigm of an individual thing as something
present in a genuine "now." The essence of phenomenological
tone-quality, tone-intensity, of color quality, of brightness, etc.,
is itself given whether the eidetic abstraction carries out its
operation on the basis of a *perception* or on that of a *realization in
imagination;* and it is *irrelevant* to either of these whether we
suppose the objects to *exist* in actuality or in some other way. The
same holds for an apprehension of essences which has to do with
various sorts of psychic data in the proper sense, e.g., judgment,
assertion, denial, perception, inference, etc. And of course it
holds also for the general states of affairs which appertain to such
universals. The realization that of two tones one is lower, the
other higher, and that this relation is asymmetrical, is developed
within "seeing." The instances must stand before our eyes, but
not necessarily in the manner of facts of perception. For a consideration of essence, perception and imagination are to be
treated exactly alike; the same essence can equally well be "seen"

‹69› in either, / or abstracted from either, and any interpolated sup-
positions about existence are irrelevant. That the perceived tone
together with its intensity, pitch, etc., *exists* in a certain sense,
that the imagined tone, to put it bluntly, the fictitious tone, *does
not exist*, that the former is obviously present in a genuine sense,
the latter not, that in the case of memory the tone is posited as
having existed rather than as existing now and is only presented
at this moment — all this belongs to another investigation. In a
consideration of essence none of this is to the point, unless that
investigation turns its attention to the presentation of just these
distinctions, which also are capable of being given, and to establishing general principles concerning them.

Moreover it is quite clear that even if the underlying instances
are given in perception, the actual existence which sets perceptual
givenness off from other kinds has no bearing on the matter. It is
not just that imagination is as suitable as perception for the
consideration of essence; it is also the case that imagination appears to contain *individual data* within itself, and even actually
evident data.

Let us consider *mere imagination*, even without this being
fixed in memory. An imagined color is not a datum in the way a
sensed color is. We distinguish the imagined color from the
mental process of imagining the color. The hovering of the color
before me (to put it roughly) is a "now," a presently existing
cogitatio, but the color itself is not a presently existing color; it is
not perceived. On the other hand, it is given in a certain way, it
stands before my gaze. Just like the perceived color it can be
reduced through the exclusion of all transcendent significance, so
that it no longer signifies for me the color of the paper, the house,
etc. It is possible here too to refrain from positing the existence of
anything empirical; in that case I consider it just exactly as I
"see" it, or, as it were, "live" it. But in spite of that it is not a
genuine part of the mental process of imagining; it is not a present, but a presented color. It stands, *as it were*, before our eyes,
but not as a genuine presence. But with all this, it is "seen" and
as "seen" it is, in a certain sense, given. Thus I do not take it to
be a physical or psychical *existent*. Nor do I take it to be existent
in the sense of a proper *cogitatio*, which is a genuine "now," a
datum which is, as a matter of evidence, characterized as given

now. / Still, the fact that the imagined color is not given in this or ‹70›
that sense does not mean that it is given in no sense. It appears
and in appearing presents itself in such a way that "seeing" it
itself in its presentation I can make judgments concerning the
abstract aspects which constitute it and the ways in which these
aspects cohere. Naturally these are also given in the same sense,
and likewise they do not "actually" exist anywhere in the mental
process of imagining. They are not genuinely present; they are
only "represented." The pure judgment of imagination, the mere
expression of the *content*, the specific essence of that which
appears, can assert: this is found in this way, contains these
aspects, is changed in such and such a way — without saying
anything at all about existence as really involved in objective
time, about the actual present, past, and future. We could therefore say that it is concerning the *individual essence* that we make
judgments and not concerning existence. Just on that account is
the general judgment of essence, which we usually just call the
judgment of essence, independent of the distinction between
perception and imagination. Perception posits *existence*, but it
also has an *essence* which as *content* posited as existing can also be
the same in representation.

But the contrast of *existence* and *essence* signifies nothing else
than that here two modes of being manifest themselves in two
modes of self-givenness and are to be distinguished. In merely
imagining a color, the existence which attaches to that color as
an actuality in time is not in question; no judgment is made
concerning it, and nothing concerning it is given in the *content*
of the imagination. But this color appears; it stands there; it is
a "this"; it can become the subject of a judgment, and an evident
judgment. Thus a mode of givenness is displayed in the intuitions
in imagination and the evident judgments which are grounded on
them. To be sure, if we restrict ourselves to the sphere of particular individuals, then we can hardly get started with this kind of
judgment. Only if we construct general judgments of essence,
can we attain the secure objectivity which science demands. But
that does not matter here. Hence we seem to get into a pretty
kettle of fish.

The earliest stage was the *evidence of the cogitatio*. There it
seemed first of all as if we were on solid ground — / *being pure and* ‹71›

simple. Here one would only have to grasp and "see" it. That one could, in reflecting on these data, compare and distinguish, that one could separate out the specific universals and so put forward judgments of essence, all this could be easily managed. But now it becomes clear that the pure being of the *cogitatio* reveals itself, on closer inspection, to be something which is not as simple as all that. It becomes clear that in the Cartesian sphere itself *different types* of objectivity are "constituted." And to say that they are constituted implies that immanent data are not, as it first seemed, simply in consciousness in the sense in which things are in a box, but that all the time they are displayed in something like "appearances." These appearances neither are nor genuinely contain the objects themselves. Rather in their shifting and remarkable structure they create objects in a certain way for the ego, insofar as appearances of just such a sort and just such a construction belong to that in which what we call "givenness" has been lying all along.

The *primary temporal object* is constituted in perception, along with the retention of consciousness of what is perceived; only in that sort of consciousness can time be given. Thus the universal is constituted in the *consciousness of universality* which is built up from perception and imagination. The content of intuition, in the sense of a particular *essence,* is constituted in either imagination or perception indifferently, while abstracting from existential claims. And, to remind you of this right away, from this proceed the categoreal acts, which are always presupposed in any evident assertions. The categoreal forms which we encounter here, which find expression in words like "is" and "not," "same" and "other," "one" and "many," "and" and "or," and in the forms of predication and attribution, etc., point to the forms of thinking by means of which thought-forms, when they have been appropriately constructed, come to consciousness on the basis of synthetic data which tie together the simplest acts: states of affairs of this and that ontological form. It is also at this point that the "self-constitution" of the actual objects takes place in the cognitive acts which have been so formed. The consciousness in which the given object as well as the pure "seeing" of things is brought to fulfillment is, however, not like an empty box in
<72> which these / data are simply lying; it is the *"seeing" conscious-*

ness, which, apart from attention, consists of mental acts which are *formed in such and such ways;* and the things which are not mental acts are nevertheless constituted in these acts, and come to be given in such acts. It is only as so constituted that they display themselves as what they are.

But is this not an absolute marvel? And where does this constituting of objects begin and where does it end? Are there any actual limits to it? Isn't it true that in every representation or judgment we get at a datum in a certain sense? Isn't each object a datum, and an evident datum, just insofar as it is intuited, represented, or thought in such and such a way? In the perception of an external thing, just that thing, let us say a house standing before our eyes, is said to be perceived. The house is a transcendent thing, and forfeits its existence after the phenomenological reduction. The house-appearance, this *cognitatio,* emerging and disappearing in the stream of consciousness, is given as actually evident. In this house-phenomenon we find a phenomenon of redness, of extension, etc. These are evident data. But is it not also evident that a house appears in the house-phenomenon, and that it is just on that account that we call it a perception of a house? And what appears is not only a house in general, but just exactly this house, determined in such and such a way and appearing in that determination. Can I not make an evidently true judgment as follows: on the basis of the appearance or in the content of this perception, the house is thus and so, a brick building, with a slate roof, etc.?

And if I give free rein to fantasy, so that, e.g., perhaps I see a knight like St. George killing a dragon, is it not evident that the fantasy-phenomenon represents precisely St. George, and even St. George as described in such and such a way, and that thus it here represents something transcendent? Can I not make evident judgments here, not about the genuine content of the appearance in fantasy, but about the object which appears? To be sure, only one aspect of the object comes within the purview of this realization in imagination, although more and more aspects can be brought therein; but nevertheless it is still evident that this object, this knight St. George, lies within the meaning of the phenomenon, and is manifested there "as a datum" of a sort proper to appearance.

<73>   And finally we come to so-called *symbolic thinking*. Let us say
that without any intuition I think that 2 times 2 equals 4. Can I
doubt that I have directed my thought to this arithmetical
proposition and that what is thought does not concern, e.g.,
today's weather? If this is evidently so, is there not also something functioning as a datum here? And if we go this far, nothing
can prevent us from recognizing that the paradoxical, the
completely absurd, is also "given" in a certain way. A round
square does not appear in imagination as a dragon killer appears
to me, nor does it appear in perception as an arbitrary external
thing; but an intentional object is still obviously there. I can
describe the phenomenon, "thinking of a round square," in
terms of its genuine content. The round square itself cannot be
found there, and still it is evident that it is thought in this mental
act and that in the object so thought roundness and squareness
as such are thought. In other words, the object of this thought is
both round and square.

Above all, it must not be said that the data to which we have
finally been led in these considerations are actual data in the
true sense; in that case everything perceived, imagined, pretend-
ed, or symbolically thought, every fiction and absurdity, would
be "evidently given." But all that would be indicated by all this
would be that *great difficulties are involved here*. It cannot hinder
us in our quest for enlightenment to hold fast to the principle:
givenness extends just as far as actual evidence. But of course the
basic question will be this. In the achievement of pure evidence
what is actually given in it and what is not? What is it that is
produced therein only be an alien mode of thought? What
interpretations are introduced without any basis in the data
themselves?

And in general it is not primarily a matter of clinging to certain
selected appearances as data, but rather of getting insight into
the nature of givenness and of the self-constitution of different
modes of objectivity. Certainly each mental phenomenon has its
relation to objects; and (this is the most fundamental fact
about it) each has its genuine (*reellen*) content, which is a *belief* [1]
in those aspects which compose it in the genuine sense. But on
the other hand there is its intentional object, an object which it

[1] English in the original.

intends to constitute in such and such a way according to its essential kind.

In order to bring this matter to actual evidence, we must get <74> everything we need from the evidence itself. Within it we must become clear as to what this "intentional inexistence" really signifies and how it is related to the genuine content of the mental phenomenon. We must see in what connections it appears as actual and proper evidence, and what in these connections actual and proper givenness is. We will then be in a position to *set forth the different modes of givenness in the proper sense, and likewise the constitution of different modes of objectivity and their relations to one another:* the givenness of the *cogitatio,* the givenness of the *cogitatio preserved in a fresh recollection,* the givenness of the *unity of appearance* enduring in the phenomenal flux, the givenness of *change* itself, the givenness of *things* to the "outer" sense, the givenness of the different forms of imagination and memory, as well as the givenness of *perceptions* and other sorts of *representations* which unify themselves synthetically in many ways in fitting associations. Of course there is also *logical givenness,* the givenness of *universals,* of *predicates,* of *states of affairs,* etc.; also the givenness of *something absurd,* of *something contradictory,* of *something which does not exist.* In general, whether a datum manifests what is merely represented or what truly exists, what is real or what is ideal, what is possible or what is impossible, it is *a datum in the cognitive phenomenon,* in the phenomenon of a thought, in the widest sense of the term. And, *generally speaking, it is in the consideration of essences that this correlation, which seems so wonderful at first sight, is to be investigated.*

It is only in cognition that the essence of objectivity can be studied at all, with respect to all its basic forms; only in cognition is it truly given, is it evidently "seen." This *evident "seeing"* itself is truly *cognition in the fullest sense.* And the object is not a thing which is put into cognition as into a sack, as if cognition were a completely empty form, one and the same empty sack in which now this, now / that is placed. But in givenness we see *that the* <75> *object is constituted in cognition,* that a number of different basic forms of objectivity are to be distinguished, as well as an equal number of different forms of the given cognitive acts and of clusters and interconnections of cognitive acts. And cognitive acts, more generally any metal acts, are not isolated particulars, coming and going in the stream of consciousness without any interconnections. As they are essentially related to one another, they display a teleological *coherence* and corresponding connections of realization, corroboration, verification, and their opposites. And on these connections, which present an intelligible unity, a great deal depends. They themselves are involved in the constitution of objects. They logically bring together acts which are and acts which are not given in the proper sense, acts of mere representation (or rather of mere belief) and acts of insight. And they bring together the multiplicity of acts which are relative to this same objectivity, whether they take place in intuitive or in nonintuitive thought.

And it is in these interconnections that the objectivity involved in the objective sciences is first constituted, not in one stroke but in a gradually ascending process — and especially the objectivity of real spatio-temporal actuality.

All this is to be investigated, and investigated in the sphere of pure evidence, in order to throw light on the great problems of the nature of cognition and the meaning of the *correlation of cognition and the object of cognition.* Originally the problem concerned *the relation between subjective psychological experience and the actuality grasped therein, as it is in itself* — first of all actual reality, and then also the mathematical and other sorts of ideal realities. But first we need the insight that the *crucial problem* must rather have to do with the *relation between cognition and its object,* but in the *reduced* sense, according to which we are dealing not with human cognition, but with cognition in general, apart from any existential assumptions either of the empirical ego or of <76> a real world. We need the insight that the truly significant / problem is that of the *ultimate bearing of cognition,* including the problem of objectivity in general, which only is what it is in correlation with possible cognition. Further, we need the insight that this problem can only be solved within the sphere of pure evidence, the sphere of data which are ultimate norms because they are absolutely given. And finally we need the realization that we must then investigate one by one, by the strict process of "seeing," all the fundamental forms of cognition and of the objects which fully or partially attain givenness within cognition, in order to determine the meaning of all the correlations which have to be explicated.